On behalf of Crown Limited we'd like to take this opportunity to extend our congratulations to Ansett Australia as it celebrates its 65th anniversary. Ansett Australia continues to provide outstanding service and is at the forefront in the Australian aviation industry.

Crown is the largest and most diverse entertainment resort of its kind in the world. Located on the south bank of Melbourne's Yarra River, it is the outstanding entertainment venue in Australia and Victoria's most visited tourist destination.

The complex features Crown Casino, which has 2500 gaming machines and 350 gaming tables, making it the largest casino in the southern hemisphere. Crown also features Melbourne's most luxurious hotel – Crown Towers; Australia's biggest ballroom – the Palladium; 50 restaurants, brasseries, bistros and bars; three nightclubs; 14 cinemas, a theatre and the most extensive collection of exclusive international designer labels under one roof.

Crown Towers specialises in catering to the business traveller and corporate guest. These guests are able to further enjoy the luxury, comfort and privacy of the Crystal Club, an exclusive lounge facility located on level 29.

Some of Melbourne's finest dining establishments can be found at Crown, such as Koko and Silks, Breezes, JJ's Bar & Grill and Conservatory. Crown's chefs are world-class leaders in their industry, making each meal at Crown a memorable dining experience.

For your next meeting at Crown, for either business or pleasure, we invite you to come and experience Crown's unparalleled level of standard and service.

To John.

Regards David

CROWN

A WORLD OF ENTERTAINMENT

dining high

STUNNING RECIPES from AUSTRALIA'S MASTER CHEFS

managing editor TONY BILSON food PETER DOYLE
photography ASHLEY BARBER styling BARBARA BECKETT

Focus Publishing Pty Ltd
ACN 003 600 360
PO Box 518 Edgecliff NSW 2027
Telephone 61 2 9327 4777
Fax 61 2 9362 3753
Email: focus@focus.com.au
Website: www.focus.com.au

Chairman: Steven Rich
Publisher: Jaqui Lane
Associate Publisher: Jenny Walkden
Project Director: William Munt
General Manager, Publishing: Mark Newman
Production Manager: Timothy Ho

Editor: Philippa Sandall
Designer: Tracey Quinn
Recipe Co-ordination: Barbara Beckett
Recipe Editing: Andrea Smith
Customer Service: Sophie Beaumont
Design Assistant: Annie Farkas

ISBN 1 875359 58 3

contents

roll of honour

major participants

The Boeing Company
Carlton & United Breweries Limited
Crown Limited
Gate Gourmet International AG
Harrison Systems Integration Pty Ltd
IBM Australia Limited
PRC-DeSoto Australia Pty Ltd
SalesForce Australia Pty Ltd
Unisys Australia Limited

key participants

The Allens Arthur Robinson Group
Ansett Air Freight
Avis Australia
Bain International
Clemenger Direct
Concorde International Travel Ltd
DMR Consulting Group (Australia) Pty Ltd
Foodservice Equipment International Pty Limited
George Patterson Bates
Hotel Enterprize
LINK Recruitment Group
Maddock Lonie & Chisholm Lawyers
Memorex Telex Asia-Pacific
Morgan & Banks Limited
Nortel Networks
PAC Australia Pty Ltd
Salmat Pty Ltd
Seven Network Limited

contributing participants

AAV Business Communications
Accor
Airbus Industrie
Air Canada
Ansett Australia Chauffeur Drive
Australian Cricket Board
Australian Football League
Berri Limited
Bliss-Fox Ground Support Equipment Pty Limited
Boyer Group Pty Ltd
Caltex Australia Limited
Centrepoint Properties / EH Larmar & Co
Com Tech Communications Pty Ltd
Connat Flight Services Pty Ltd
De Bortoli Wines Pty Limited
Dowd Corporation Pty Ltd
Feltex Carpets Limited
Group 4 Securitas Pty Limited
Hamilton Island Enterprises Pty Ltd
Hawker de Havilland Components Pty Limited
Hayman
Hewlett-Packard Australia Limited
Hilton Hotels
Hotel Lindrum
Hyatt Hotels & Resorts
Long Gully Estate
Long Prosper Enterprise Co. Ltd
Lyncroft Consulting Group
Mission Personnel Services Pty Ltd
National Rugby League
Nutters Foods Pty Ltd
QBE Insurance (Australia) Limited
Senteq Information Systems
Sydney Airports Corporation Ltd
Westralia Airports Corporation Pty Ltd
WT Partnership

The YEAR 2000 is a SPECIAL one for Ansett Australia. The company is CELEBRATING 65 YEARS of providing outstanding service to Australian travellers and flies into the new millennium with renewed VIGOUR and confidence as the OFFICIAL AIRLINE of the Sydney 2000 OLYMPIC GAMES. And as a member of the Star Alliance network, Ansett is now the Australian GATEWAY to the LARGEST AIRLINE network in the WORLD, affording customers an unparallelled range of INTEGRATED SERVICES right around the world.

Anniversaries are important for many reasons, but especially because they provide us with the chance to remember how it all began, to reflect on our proud heritage and to look positively ahead to the challenges and changes that the future will bring. During this exciting time our core values and key business strategies remain firmly in place. We are committed to working with our business partners to continually improve our customer service; to be the airline that is renowned worldwide for the quality of its people and its product.

We are very aware of the challenges that lie ahead and have positioned the airline to exploit the best opportunities for our customers through technology, aircraft choice and engine type, cost control and service enhancements that will ensure Ansett Australia is right at the top of the list of the world's great airlines.

Challenge in fact was something that the company's founder, Reg Ansett, absolutely thrived on. Sixty-five years ago, in 1935, Reg Ansett was unable to renew his road operating licences under newly introduced State Government legislation prohibiting road services from competing with Victoria's railways. But he had his pilot's licence and a De Havilland Gypsy Moth aircraft and

decided to register the name Ansett Airways. He recruited his first pilot, Vern Cerche, and his first engineer, John Davies. He then bought a Porterfield VH-UVH, ran a flying school, barnstormed and flew around properties in Victoria selling Ansett Airways shares to the local pastoralists. On 26 December 1935 he bought his first commercial aircraft, a single-engine Fokker F-X1 Universal for £1000. The spare engine came later.

On 17 February 1936, Ansett Airways made its first flight from Hamilton to Melbourne, the beginning of a regular weekday service. Later in the year, Reg Ansett added an eight-seat Airspeed Envoy to his fleet (with the help of £500 prize money from winning the handicap section of the Brisbane–Adelaide air race in the Porterfield VH-UVH with his brother Jack), and the Hamilton–Sydney service took off.

In its first year of service, Ansett Airways flew 895,983 miles and carried 12,624 passengers.

Sixty-five years on the Ansett fleet consists of 70 aircraft with 423 daily departures and services to 95 destinations in eight countries. With its links to the Star Alliance airlines, Ansett Australia can offer its customers a network covering 720 destinations in over 110 countries.

Today Ansett Australia is one of the world's oldest operating airlines, proudly serving travellers in Australia and around the world as a member of the Star Alliance network. The company is positioned to achieve significant passenger growth in the new millennium thanks to the interline traffic generated through the Star Alliance network and its other partnering agreements. Ansett Australia's business and that of its key suppliers will increase exponentially.

These international linkages coupled with Ansett's status as the official airline of the Sydney 2000 Olympic Games will kickstart passenger growth in 2000 and provide Ansett with worldwide exposure on an unprecedented scale.

Our 65th anniversary provides us with a way to mark these exciting developments, to commemorate them in a way that is uniquely Australian, uniquely Ansett and that recognises the excellence that has become synonymous with Ansett. With this beautiful book we invite our readers to be our guest on a taste-tempting culinary journey that features recipes from Australia's celebrity chefs, from our own award-winning chefs and from the executive chefs of our Star Alliance partners.

ANSETT AUSTRALIA

introduction

be our guest

The CULINARY JOURNEY you are about to undertake CELEBRATES Ansett Australia's 65th anniversary with recipes from celebrity chefs. As Ansett is world renowned for its EXCELLENCE, so too are these chefs HONOURED locally and internationally for their contribution to Australian cuisine.

—Tony Bilson

It was the inability of Australia's early settlers to adjust to local food sources that first defined the direction of Australian cooking. Those who came to New South Wales with the First Fleet nearly starved waiting for their supplies of salted beef, flour and tea from Britain, when they were surrounded by one of the most unspoiled and abundant natural food-producing environments in the world.

The history of cooking in Australia reflects the development of Australian society, from the arrival of the first British and Irish settlers to the fortune-seekers from around the world who came with the gold rushes, the European refugees arriving post-World War II, the more recent Asian migrants since the 1970s and the belated accommodation with the Aborigines.

From its humble beginnings of salted beef, flour and tea, the food the colonists ate improved as the colony's wealth grew, particularly once gold was discovered. Wines were imported from France, Spain and Portugal, European game was introduced, and rabbits, deer, foxes and hare soon found their way onto the plates of the

colonists. Soon they were able to replicate the world they had left behind.

Classic French dining established itself in the grand hotels, and trains travelling to the goldfields featured elaborate menus with first-growth burgundies and clarets on their wine lists. The major champagne houses sold more of their wine to Australia than to anywhere else in the world during the gold rush decades, and their principals made the long journey by ship to look after this market. Bollinger used to send free bottles to the discoverers of major strikes to ensure that their wine was always synonymous with success and great wealth.

Perhaps the longest-lasting culinary influence, however, was the Chinese. Throughout the 20th century, Chinese food was the most popular exotic dining experience in Australia. It is no accident that Adelaide's famous chef, Cheong Liew, is in the avant garde of Australian cuisine and the Flower Drum is widely regarded as Melbourne's best restaurant.

With Federation came investment in manufacturing industries, the motor car and the aeroplane. It also brought an early combination of creativity and knowhow to water conservation and irrigation, which turned the desolate plains of the New South Wales south-west into the richly fertile Riverina area. This area soon became the base for some of the best in Australian fruit and vegetables.

From a culinary point of view, the 1940s was a great time for gourmet appetites, with grand restaurants and hotels catering for the wealthy and the ambitious. I remember the two Hotels Australia (in Melbourne and in Sydney) catering for the smart set. The Windsor Hotel was the grand dame of Melbourne, where wealthy wool growers and traders dined cheek by jowl with politicians.

In the 1950s, Mario's Restaurant and the Florentino were established in Melbourne; Romanos was the place to be seen in Sydney and Allens Fish Cafes catered for the workers. My parents' hotel in Liverpool had a dining room where trout and game were regularly on the menu. Many country towns had a grand hotel with a dining room which usually served competently cooked English dishes.

The winemakers started to become more confident. Maurice O'Shea had returned from France and made some classic wines that helped define Hunter Valley styles. Max Schubert was later to imitate his experience and to make Grange for Penfolds. The market expanded. The Wynns in Melbourne and the Walkers in Sydney opened wine bars where even respectable people could go and be seen. Len Evans continued this grand tradition at Bulletin Place, Sydney, during the 1970s. Today the grand tradition is maintained by Jimmy Watson's in Melbourne's Carlton and the Universal Wine Bar in Adelaide.

When all these factors are combined with the post-war immigration from Europe and the multitude of culinary skills and influences it brought with it, it is evident that Australia experienced a culinary revolution comparable in its impact to the arrival of the tomato and potato in 16th century Europe.

This revolution acquired a sophisticated overlay when chefs were imported to cope with the Olympic Games in Melbourne in 1956. A young Swiss chef, Hermann Schneider, was later to open his own world-famous restaurant, Two Faces, and the Wynns backed a debonair French immigrant, Georges Mora, and his wife Mirka into a restaurant that I still remember with awe – Balzac.

Balzac was Australia's first contemporary restaurant. Artists mixed with the social set, wines were served by the glass, the asparagus was fresh and the vinaigrette had no sugar. The jugged hare was pungent and powerful and when I tasted it with the Wynns Ovens Valley Burgundy, I was bound for gastronomic heaven. And a career as a chef.

JK Walker in Sydney had opened his Rhine Castle Bistro, headquarters for the Wine and Food Society. The kitchen was run by the fine chef Paul Harbulot and his Sous Chef Jean Ansourian. Here was classic and Provençale cooking at its best with a cellar of Australian and French wines unmatched in the country. JK, as he was known, was a devotee of Hunter wine, and with his partner Harry Brown he formed the circle of gastronomes which took Australian cooking into the 1960s. Margaret Fulton taught cooking in the Bistro, watched by a thin young cook (me) who eagerly soaked up any advice thrown his way. Elizabeth David's classic *French Provincial Cooking* was a bestseller, and Ted Moloney wrote a small classic, *Oh, for a French Wife!*.

The Italians and Greeks had begun to make their mark, not only in the grand restaurants but more pervasively in the small cafes and suburbs they claimed as their own. Yugoslavian grill cafes were popular – the Balkan Restaurant in Oxford Street is now one of Sydney's oldest restaurants. Middle Eastern cooking was championed by the Lebanese and Turks. Central European cooking included Czechoslovak and Hungarian fare, and Polish and German cafes sprang up and were also dominant in the Australian ski fields.

In post-war France there was a new revolution too, led by Fernand Point in Vienne, Alexandre Dumain in Burgundy and Raymond Oliver in Paris. The foundations were laid for contemporary cooking as it is today, and the generation of chefs produced by these kitchens were to be celebrated internationally. The age of media meant that they influenced cooking globally. Paul Bocuse, Michel Guèrard, the Troisgros brothers, Alain Chapel, Jacques Manière, Louis Outhier, Alain Pic and Roger Vergé – these stars of modern French cooking seemed to be in every magazine, given the highest honours and almost on their own made France the most popular tourist destination in the world.

Many of them came and cooked in Australia. Of these chefs the most influential has proved to be Michel Guèrard. The way he plated food still looks as fresh today as it did 25 years ago. He altered the way we looked at and tasted food. We were never to return to the classic look of Escoffier or even Fernand Point.

My partner Gay and I started a small bistro, Tony's Bon Gout, in Elizabeth Street, Sydney in May 1973. It was unlicensed (BYO) and a three-course meal could be had for $4.50. We cooked classic French food but the sauces were unthickened with flour. We searched for new ingredients, fresh herbs, we baked our own bread, made our own pastry. When Leo Schofield gave us a rave review, suddenly we were booked out up to four months in advance. Our head waiter, Alain Chagny, was from Beaujolais. His father had fought with Fernand Point in the Resistance, and when we made our first trip to France the Chagny family introduced us to all of the great chefs.

It was encouraging to find that the direction we had taken was also the view of the French. We took classic dishes and recreated them in a contemporary idiom. Alain Chapel was my main inspiration. He took his local cooking of the Dombes area and transported it to create a cuisine that was poetic and elegant.

The media played an important part in this development. Len Evans, Sam Orr, Neville Baker, Leo Schofield and Margaret Fulton all wrote regularly on food and restaurants. Leo Schofield was the unchallenged doyen of restaurant critics. He had visited many of the finest restaurants internationally and held their vision in high esteem. Leo was excited by the devotion to excellence and the high experience they offered. He conveyed his enthusiasm to a wide audience through his columns and helped create a demand for fine food.

The 1970s and 1980s saw Australia accepting migrants from southern Asia. The Thai, Vietnamese, Malay and Indian communities strengthened and formed part of Australian society and, like the earlier European immigrants, opened cafes and restaurants. More importantly, their cooking appealed to a wide audience and was promoted through the media. Today the use of Asian ingredients is commonplace in Australian cuisine – not as a manufactured fusion cuisine, but as a natural part of our everyday culinary experience.

Perhaps one of the most important qualities of modern Australian cooking is the assimilation of different culinary influences. It is this phenomenon that has created a defining moment in the development of our cuisine and strongly differentiates it from other international contemporary cuisines.

Great cooking can inspire and touch us in a way that is different from literature or the visual arts because the experience is ephemeral and individual. We cooks do not have to burn our bad manuscripts to preserve our reputation. Our reputation exists only in the memories of our diners.

AUSTRALIAN CUISINE in all its DIVERSITY is the HERO of this book CELEBRATING ANSETT'S 65TH ANNIVERSARY. I hope readers will want to enjoy their own culinary JOURNEY, either in their home kitchen or by visiting Australia's SUPERB food and wine-growing regions where they can DELIGHT in the FARE of Australia's celebrity chefs FIRSTHAND, either on the ground or in the air.

wine

Tony Bilson's EVOCATIVE and DETAILED introduction to the historical development of GASTRONOMY in Australia makes my task much easier. Taking a BIRD'S EYE VIEW, there have been three distinct stages in the DEVELOPMENT of the WINE INDUSTRY.

—*James Halliday, Ansett's wine consultant*

The first covers the period from 1823 (when Gregory Blaxland exported the first wine to England) to 1901, the year of Federation. During this time, vines spread across the southern half of Australia: metropolitan Sydney, the Hunter Valley and Mudgee (New South Wales); virtually the whole of Victoria; Hobart (briefly); the Barossa, Eden and Clare Valleys and McLaren Vale (South Australia); and the Swan Valley (Western Australia).

The discovery of gold injected great wealth into the community as a whole from the mid 1850s until 1893, when the bank crash and depression brought an abrupt end to the days of wine and roses. But by this time a thriving industry, with a strong export focus, had been established particularly of lusty red wines, which doctors in both Australia and the United Kingdom were happy to prescribe for the health of anaemic or otherwise sickly patients. Much was table wine, and all of the classic grape varieties of France were propagated in various parts of Australia, including cool climate regions.

Federation removed interstate tariff barriers at the very time that the irrigation areas along the Murrumbidgee and Murray rivers were being established. With a sizeable boost from soldier settlement schemes in the years after World War I, and the first influx of Italian migrants, production of cheap fortified wine became the driving force of the industry. In the 1920s, exports of fortified wine to the United Kingdom reached a level not seen again until the late 1980s.

Thus it was that during the second period between 1901 and 1955 that the whole focus of the industry was on fortified wine, chiefly for export but between 1940 and 1955 for domestic consumption during a time of beer rationing. Great table wine was made by a few legendary craftsman such as Colin Preece, Maurice O'Shea, Bill Redman and Roger Warren, but it represented less than 5 per cent (indeed, probably less than 1 per cent) of total production.

The third period began in 1955, and continues to this day. First Max Schubert revolutionised the approach to red winemaking; and Orlando and Yalumba that of white winemaking, and in particular, riesling. Then, in the 1970s, there came the simultaneous expansion of the industry into cool climate regions (in many instances those which had flourished in the 19th century, such as the Yarra Valley) and the planting (or replanting) of varieties such as chardonnay, pinot noir, merlot and cabernet sauvignon.

Concurrently with these developments, domestic wine consumption grew from around 6 litres per capita at the start of the 1960s (even then, much of it fortified) to over 21 litres per capita in 1987, by far the largest in the English-speaking world. This growth was pushed by the introduction of a technologically perfect wine cask in the early 1970s, which dramatically changed the socio-economic profile of the average wine drinker.

By now the changes were coming thick and fast. In 1985, exports amounted to around 8 million litres worth $21 million; by 1987 they had grown to 21 million litres worth $44 million. Ten years later the figure was 154 litres worth $603 million; two years later (by the end of 1999) they had soared to over 230 million litres worth $1.15 billion.

However, even this increase pales into insignificance with the estimated jump to 400 million litres by 2003 which will be driven by the increase in vineyards from 62,400 hectares in bearing in 1995 to 95,000 hectares in bearing by June 2002.

Yet these figures tell only half the tale. Since 1985 there has been a radical shift in emphasis encapsulated in the catch phrase 'Drinking less, but drinking better'. The once almighty cask is steadily losing ground to wine in bottle, and the bottled wine segment itself has changed dramatically.

The 1990s will be long remembered as the decade of red wine; through a conjunction of events, it has become the focus of attention of wine consumers from Shanghai to London, from Sydney to New York. Through sheer luck, Australia entered the decade with the largest plantings of old vine shiraz (100 years old or even more) in the world. Even today, its plantings are second only to those of France, and have provided Australia with its internationally recognised icons of Penfolds Grange and Henschke Hill of Grace.

These wines are as rich and generous as any in the world; when the typical Australian chardonnay is taken into account, it is not hard to see why Australian wine is often described as sunshine in a bottle.

The vast size of the continent, the unparalleled diversity of climate and site, the absence of pollution and generally low urban pressure all contribute to the dazzling array of wine styles. These range from finest sparkling wines to delicate rieslings, succulent chardonnays, stylish, intense pinot noirs, great shirazs, multi-layered cabernet sauvignons, fine sherries and ultimately to the unique, luscious, fortified muscats and tokays (of north-east Victoria).

Underlying these wines are winemaking skills honed to a fine edge by a combination of world-class research and tertiary education facilities on the one hand, and by the typically pragmatic and hard-working nature of Australian winemakers on the other. It is no accident that Australia's 'flying winemakers' are sought by wineries large and small, famous and obscure, across the great winemaking countries of Europe.

Partly as a consequence of this overseas experience, but also thanks to Australia's highly sophisticated wine show system, our winemakers are constantly seeking to refine Australia's wines and wine styles, to make them more subtle yet more intense. Whether you pay $10 or $100 for a bottle, you are entitled to expect great value for your money – and sheer pleasure from every glass.

Below: Long Gully Estate's vineyard produces premium table wines.

beer & food

It is worth remembering that some FOODS LOVE BEER. From SPARKLING lagers to CREAMY stouts, from TANGY bitters to CRISP cold-filtered beers, from light FRUITY ELEGANCE to those with CHOCOLATY overtones, there are BEERS that can COMPLEMENT EVERY COURSE.

The wine buff talks of acidity, tartness, bitterness, earthiness, fruitiness, roundness, viscosity. So too the beer buff. In addition, beer is aromatic, varies greatly in sweetness and in the depth of its bitterness, quantified by the amount of hops the brewer chooses to add.

Beer has the added flavour component of malt, nuttiness, degree of caramelisation (Carlton Draught), effervescence, and occasionally, as with wheat beers (Redback Original), clove-like, spicy qualities. The new generation beers (Carlton Cold, Foster's LightIce) are somewhat gentler, the great classics (Carlton Draught) more austere, and the differences between the pale ales and the heavier, roasted, malty styles (Dogbolter) as different as night and day.

Traditional beer-drinking nations developed cuisines that were compatible with their favourite beverage. German sausages and smoked goods go well with pilsener; British herrings – and fish and chips – with pale ale; stout with oysters and Welsh rarebit, also taking a bow with rich fruity desserts and Christmas pudding. The French developed terrines and country pâtés to serve with a glass of beer in their brasseries, which originally were eating houses attached to the great breweries of France.

The Danes enjoy their smorgasbord, prawns, gravelax and nutty-style cheeses with beer, the Flemish their mussels and chips, the northern French their carbonnades, the Americans their crab cakes and blackened catfish. The Indians, Thais and Singaporeans are beer lovers, too, because beer sits well with curries and spicy food. Beer is ideal to cleanse and refresh the palate.

Lighter beers tend to go best with the early part of a meal – light in colour, in alcohol, and in complexity of flavour. For a fish course that's pan-fried with strong herbs, capsicum, macadamias, or extra virgin olive oil – try placing a wedge of lemon in the neck of a Corona. Bring on the chicken and the meat courses, and it is time to opt for a headier, full-bodied beer with more flavour such as Crown Lager.

There are also beers elegant enough for the dessert end of a menu. The compatibility of food and beer is not necessarily confined to the two having similar qualities. Many a marriage is based on contrast. The key is simple – think of the flavours, then apply your personal taste.
—Diane Holuigue

foods that love beers

	Carlton Cold	Carlton Draught	Carlton Midstrength	Carlton Premium Dry	Cascade Premium	Cascade Premium Light	Crown Lager	Foster's LightIce	Matilda Bay Premium	Victoria Bitter
	✓	✓	✓	✓			✓	✓		✓
antipasto	✓		✓	✓			✓	✓	✓	
apple pie				✓			✓			
barbecued meats, including chicken	✓	✓					✓	✓	✓	✓
beef, Béarnaise sauce					✓					
beef, corned									✓	✓
beef, roasted			✓		✓			✓		
beef, smoked or air dried	✓		✓	✓						
beef, Thai beef salad	✓							✓		
Cajun		✓	✓					✓		
casseroles, lighter sauces	✓				✓			✓		
casseroles, richly sauced							✓		✓	✓
cheese, blue										
cheese, Cheddar	✓							✓		✓
cheese, Gruyère				✓	✓			✓		
cheese, marinated fetta	✓						✓			
cheese, Tilsit				✓				✓		
chicken, poached or roasted				✓			✓	✓		
chilli flavours								✓	✓	
Chinese							✓	✓	✓	
East meets West				✓				✓	✓	
fish and chips (fish in batter)		✓					✓	✓		
fish, creamy sauces					✓		✓	✓		
fish, smoked salmon				✓			✓	✓		
fish, smoked trout				✓						
fish, whiting							✓	✓		
Greek		✓	✓				✓			
ham (and other smoked smallgoods)	✓		✓	✓				✓		
hamburger		✓							✓	✓
Indian (curry)	✓						✓			
Japanese				✓	✓			✓		

foods that love beers

	Carlton Cold	Carlton Draught	Carlton Midstrength	Carlton Premium Dry	Cascade Premium	Cascade Premium Light	Crown Lager	Foster's LightIce	Matilda Bay Premium	Victoria Bitter
	✓	✓	✓	✓	✓		✓	✓		✓
lamb, barbecued or grilled	✓	✓			✓					
lamb, roast		✓			✓					
Lebanese	✓	✓	✓				✓		✓	
lobster				✓	✓	✓		✓		
Malaysian		✓			✓					
Mediterranean	✓							✓		
Mexican		✓	✓				✓	✓		
Moroccan		✓	✓				✓		✓	
mussels, marinière								✓		
olives	✓									
onions, pickled										✓
oysters								✓	✓	
pasta, marinara/seafood		✓		✓			✓			
pasta, strong tomato, Bolognese			✓	✓						
pâté	✓	✓	✓							
pesto								✓		
pork, roast or chops								✓	✓	
prawns, sauce tartare	✓	✓	✓				✓	✓		
puddings, steamed					✓	✓				
salad, composed (light)								✓		
salami, strong, smoked	✓		✓					✓	✓	
sauerkraut		✓							✓	✓
sausages, barbecued	✓		✓							✓
seafood					✓	✓	✓	✓		
steak		✓					✓		✓	✓
steak and kidney pie								✓		✓
tandoori	✓		✓				✓			
Thai		✓					✓	✓	✓	
veal, roast/schnitzel								✓	✓	
Vietnamese		✓					✓	✓		

myth

One of the great myths about beer is that it is fattening.

It is not.

A 200 ml glass of beer contains fewer kilojoules than a similar sized glass of red or white wine, a mixed drink, soft drink or fruit juice.

Left: Roast rack of lamb with warm cannelini bean salad served with Crown Lager, winner of the Best Premium Beer at the Australian Liquor Industry Awards.

Right: Cascade Premium makes a wonderful marriage with this warm salad of tandoori prawns.

summer

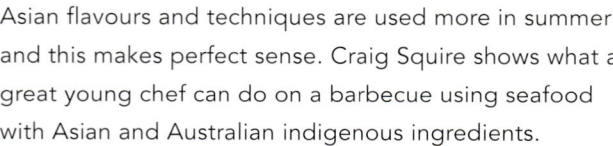

summer

Summer is HOLIDAY time. The kitchen staff spend HALF their time in the coolroom finding any excuse to ESCAPE the HEAT. Restaurants eschew the long-cooked stocks. Instead they serve LIGHT vinaigrettes and PAN SAUCES: the hallmarks of SUMMER COOKING.

—*Tony Bilson*

Asian flavours and techniques are used more in summer and this makes perfect sense. Craig Squire shows what a great young chef can do on a barbecue using seafood with Asian and Australian indigenous ingredients.

My hero, Phillip E Muskett, was a 19th century doctor who wrote *The Art of Living in Australia* in 1890. He recommended that Australians use more olive oil, cook their vegetables less, and drink wine with their food. Muskett reasoned that cultures that had formed in climates similar to Australia's had developed diets suited to their environment and that we should look to them for inspiration rather than trying to impose a cold climate diet on what is for the most part a Mediterranean or subtropical environment. It took us 100 years to change.

Anders Schultz' abalone salad is a perfect example of Australia's new summer food. Light, elegant and classy. Or Timothy Fisher and Lucio Galletto's Tasmanian lobster and potato layers with basil sauce. A perfect contemporary luncheon dish in the Mediterranean style.

Dr Muskett would be pleased.

—*Tony Bilson*

The most exciting and defining thing about modern Austral an cooking is how flavours and techniques from al over the world have been absorbed to become a natural part of our cooks' everyday armoury and the eclectic way they are applied to our produce, uninhibited by any constraints of tradition or style. True regionalism is when you catch a trout and wash it down with a steely chardonnay from the hillside behind you.
—*Graeme Phillips*

I am constantly seeking new and better produce that may not be readily available in the marketplace. I like to nurture these products. Small consistent supplies of these products are not only better tasting but are easier to work with as they are truer to their natural flavours and textures.
—*Simon Fenwick*

Australia's tropical and subtropical north produce an ever increasing range of exotic tropical fruits. I like to include custard apple, rose papaya, banana and rockmelon in my fruit salad, together with freshly scooped passionfruit pulp.
—*Stephanie Alexander*

There are wonderful food-producing regions in Australia, such as the Yarra Valley in Victoria with its excellent juvenile salmon and roe and suckling lamb. Nearby Meredith Valley produces cheeses and game equal to if not surpassing those of the European regions previously emulated. The Barossa Valley in South Australia also cultivates suckling lamb, along with chicken, geese, ducks and suckling pigs.

—*David King*

Fresh food produce is one of those wonderful conversation pieces that can cross cultural boundaries. I love having the opportunity to work with Australian food and food providores. Working with quality producers, deciding with them what produce to grow, enhances the meaning of cooking. When people meet to eat, wonderful things can and do happen. A perfect Australian peach may not start a revolution – but it is sure to brighten your day.

Lifelong bonds stem from food produce, such as international seed exchanging, community and labour market projects, environmental concerns, educational interests and events like Floriade. Some of the best food I have tasted lately has been at these farmers' markets – both urban and rural, heirloom by nature, and exotic. These early morning affairs are always rewarding.

—*Trevor Bilney*

The food regions of Australia are increasing in number and quality as primary producers begin to understand the value of fine produce. This is creating a new market which is more satisfying to the producers, the chefs and the consumers. We chefs are continually on the lookout for the best quality produce, and we all endeavour to be the first. For example, here at The Loose Box in Western Australia, we make a point to use the first of the season's globe artichokes from Wanneroo, the first asparagus from nearby Stoneville and the first baby lamb from the Avon Valley.

Our close network of local producers provides us with a great deal of the specialty produce we use, such as fresh marron from Parkerville, the wonderful yabbies from Beverly, fine quality goat's cheeses from Gidgegannup, artichokes from Wanneroo, olives and olive oil from Chidlow, and specially bred pigeons from Kalamunda. But even more impressive is our fabulous seafood, with our rock lobsters from Rottnest, fresh sardines from Fremantle, scallops from Carnarvon and an abundance of fresh fish from our coastal waters.

—*Alain Fabrègues*

a summer menu

abalone salad with cucumber

and bamboo shoots tossed

in a light curry vinaigrette

◊

roasted marron from

Parkerville with citrus sauce

◊

watermelon, honeydew melon

and rockmelon granitas

wine suggestions

1997 Grosset Polish Hill

Riesling

◊

1998 Leeuwin Estate Art Series

Sauvignon Blanc

◊

1997 Mt Horrocks Cordon Cut

Riesling, Clare Valley

Pages 18–19: Lavender farm in Nabowla, Tasmania.

abalone salad with cucumber and bamboo shoots tossed in a light curry vinaigrette

serves 4   *Anders Schultz* EXECUTIVE CHEF ANSETT INTERNATIONAL

Serve this ASIAN-INFLUENCED seafood dish with crusty bread to soak up the DELICIOUS leftover JUICES. Best ENJOYED OUTDOORS in the SUN on a LAZY AFTERNOON.

wine suggestion

Grosset Polish Hill Riesling 1997. Its crisp finish and fragrant, flowery lime blossom aroma complement the abalone flavour.

beer suggestion

Cascade Premium Lager.

abalone

Australia is one of the world's biggest producers of abalone and I thought this would be a good opportunity to showcase this wonderful mollusc. Only a small portion of the abalone is actually eaten in Australia. The greenlip abalone is from Victoria.

mesclun, enough for 4
30 thin slices abalone,
   freshly cooked or canned
40 g bamboo shoots,
   fresh or tinned
   (fresh must be blanched),
   julienned
1 carrot, peeled
   and julienned
1 cup bean sprouts,
   washed
1 Lebanese cucumber,
   peeled and seeded,
   cut into thin slices
4 spring onions,
   sliced thinly diagonally
35 g shiitake mushrooms,
   julienned
2 tablespoons sesame
   seeds, lightly toasted

**LIGHT CURRY
VINAIGRETTE**
$1/2$ teaspoon salt
$1/4$ teaspoon freshly
   ground black pepper
1 teaspoon curry powder
$1/4$ cup white wine vinegar
$1/4$ cup lemon juice
2 cups virgin olive oil
$1/4$ cup abalone juice

To make the vinaigrette, place the salt, pepper and curry powder in a bowl. Add the vinegar and lemon juice and mix well. Pour in the oil and abalone juice and mix until all the ingredients are combined.

To make the abalone salad, place the mesclun and half the abalone and all the cut vegetables in a large bowl. Add the curry vinaigrette and toss gently to ensure that the soft leaves are not bruised.

To serve, place equal quantities into 4 bowls and top with the rest of the abalone. Sprinkle with the sesame seeds.

goong sarong

serves 4   *Sean Flakelar* AMANUSA RESORT BALI

Goong sarong is a light THAI PRAWN APPETISER wrapped in CRISPY fried rice noodles, and eaten with a CREAMY lemon and lime DIPPING SAUCE. Goong means PRAWN and sarong comes from the NOODLES which are wrapped around the prawn.

wine suggestion
Tim Knappstein Riesling 1994 is an excellent vintage for any Asian dish – the bouquet is fine, floral with citrus and herbal notes.

beer suggestion
Cascade Premium Lager.

Yamba prawns
The nutty flavour of the Yamba prawns marries well with the crunch of the crispy noodles and is refreshed by the citrus tang of the lemon and lime. This appetiser combines the best of Australia's seafood with a contemporary Asian flavour.

320 g fine rice noodles, Gay Seng Bhuket if available
800 g medium-sized prawns
vegetable oil for deep-frying
1–2 banana leaves
1 bunch fresh coriander, picked over

LEMON DIPPING SAUCE
2 egg yolks
$1/2$ teaspoon English mustard
1 teaspoon Maldon sea salt
white pepper to taste
1 teaspoon sugar
$2^1/2$ tablespoons olive oil
$2^1/2$ tablespoons Carnation condensed milk
$2^1/2$ tablespoons lemon juice, Lisbon Meyer if available
$2^1/2$ tablespoons lime juice, Tahitian or Mexican if available

To make the lemon dipping sauce, place the egg yolks in a small bowl along with the mustard, salt, pepper and sugar. Slowly whisk in the oil, then the condensed milk. Add the lemon and lime juices. Store in the refrigerator.

To wrap the prawns, soak the noodles in cold water for about 10 seconds, drain and place on absorbent kitchen paper. Remove the prawn heads, shell and devein. Wash thoroughly in plenty of water. Place about 15 strands of noodles in one hand and fold the top end into a bend facing down. Lay a prawn across the top of the noodles and loosely wrap noodles around the prawn, keeping only the tail showing. Repeat with the remaining prawns.

Fill a large saucepan two-thirds full of vegetable oil and heat to a medium temperature, about 170°C. Deep-fry the prawns, a few at a time, until a light golden colour. Drain on kitchen paper.

To serve, cover each serving plate with a piece of banana leaf and place the prawns in a graceful pile in the centre. Garnish with coriander leaves sprinkled over the prawns and serve with the lemon dipping sauce on the side. Eat with your fingers for maximum enjoyment!

quail with Balinese spices and cassava leaves

serves 2   *David King* BEGAWAN GIRI ESTATE BALI

wine suggestion
A light structured rosé
such as Taltarni or even
Domaine Chandon.

beer suggestion
Matilda Bay Premium.

quails

Whenever I make this dish
I like to use quails from
Luv-a-Duck in Victoria. This
farm grows their game with
great integrity. They are
producing Australia's best
pekin-style duck.

2 x 180 g quail
2 x 30 g quail eggs
vinegar
10 g cassava leaves twice
  blanched, or spinach
  plus 1 tablespoon
  tamarind water
vegetable oil for
  deep-frying
1 red shallot, sliced
  lengthways, deep-fried
1 1/2 tablespoons coconut
  cream, warmed

SPICE PASTE
4 red shallots, peeled
  and chopped
6 garlic cloves,
  peeled and chopped
2 tablespoons lemongrass,
  soft part only, finely
  sliced
6 candlenuts, chopped
1 1/2 tablespoons red
  turmeric, peeled
  and chopped
2 tablespoons ginger,
  peeled and chopped
1 1/2 tablespoons kencur
  root or 3 teaspoons
  white turmeric (optional)
2 teaspoons dried shrimp
  paste, roasted in banana
  leaf or foil
4–5 large red chillies,
  deseeded and chopped
1 cup pork fat
fish sauce to taste

CASSAVA PURÉE
40 g cassava leaves, twice
  blanched, or spinach
  plus 1 tablespoon
  tamarind water
2 teaspoons fresh ginger,
  julienned
salt to taste
3 teaspoons gula jawl
  (Indonesian dark
  palm sugar)

To make the spice paste, blend all the spice paste ingredients
together until finely ground. Sauté the paste in the pork fat in
a frying pan over a low heat until fragrant, about 30–40 minutes.
Season with the fish sauce to taste – the paste can be quite
salty so be careful not to add too much.

Preheat the oven to 250°C.

To cook the quails, rub the quails inside and out with
2–3 tablespoons of the spice paste. Plunge the quail eggs into
boiling water for 2 minutes then steep in a 2 parts vinegar to
1 part water solution for 40–60 minutes. The vinegar will break
down the calcium in the shell, allowing for easy peeling of the
soft eggs. Roughly chop the cassava leaves and fill the cavity
of the marinated birds. Then put in a quail egg so it is slightly
protruding. Heat a large saucepan one-third full of oil and when
hot, deep-fry the birds until golden, about 3 minutes. Place
them on an oven tray and finish cooking in the preheated oven
for another 2–3 minutes. Remove from the oven and let the
quails rest for 1 minute.

To make the cassava purée, combine all the purée
ingredients in a saucepan. If using the spinach, add the tamarind
water. Simmer for 10 minutes and blend in a food processor.
It should be rich, sweet and slightly bitter. Warm 2 tablespoons
of the spice paste.

To serve, spoon some of the cassava or spinach purée in the
centre of each plate. Split the birds in half lengthways and
remove the backbone. Lay the breasts on top of each other over
the cassava purée. Liberally spoon the spice paste over the
breasts. Finish by dressing the quails with a good smattering of
crisp deep-fried red shallots. Spoon the coconut cream around
the plate.

two coloured ravioli, taleggio cheese and baby spinach with truffle oil

serves 6   *Marcel Nosari* HAYMAN

tip

Make the yellow and green pasta separately, preferably the day before using. Freeze any leftover dough for another occasion.

YELLOW PASTA

1 cup water
2 teaspoons saffron threads
4 cups fine semolina flour
2 large eggs

GREEN PASTA

5 tablespoons water
200 g fresh spinach leaves
4 cups fine semolina flour
2 large eggs

TALEGGIO AND SPINACH FILLING

200 g taleggio cheese
300 g ricotta cheese
100 g fresh spinach leaves
50 g parmesan cheese
4 eggs
1 tablespoon freshly
   chopped thyme, marjoram
   and sage leaves
salt and freshly ground
   black pepper to taste

RAVIOLI TRUFFLE SAUCE

200 g butter
100 g parmesan cheese
1 tablespoon truffle oil
2 handfuls baby
   spinach leaves

2 egg yolks, beaten,
   to make the pasta block
2 eggs, beaten,
   to make the ravioli

To make yellow colouring, combine the water and saffron in a saucepan and bring to the boil. Leave to cool.

To make green colouring, wilt the spinach leaves in boiling water. Drain then purée the leaves. Cool.

To prepare yellow pasta, place the flour on the bench and form a well in the centre. Whisk the eggs gently in a bowl then pour into the well. Add the saffron colouring and gradually mix together until a dough has formed. Use your fingers or a fork. Knead the dough for about 10 minutes until it becomes satiny, smooth and very elastic. Cover with cling wrap and rest for at least 30 minutes (up to 3 hours).

Repeat with the spinach purée to make green pasta.

To prepare ravioli sheets, use a pasta machine. Divide the pasta into egg-size balls. Flatten the dough with the palm of your hand so that it fits between the rollers, about 13 mm thick. Feed the dough through the pasta machine on the widest setting. Sprinkle the resulting strip with flour and fold into thirds. Place the strips on floured tea towels as you go, making sure they do not overlap. Repeat this feeding, flouring and folding 3–5 times, until the dough is smooth and elastic and ready to be stretched. Reduce the machine settings gradually and continue to roll out the pasta until it is 3 mm thick. Roll sheets through the finer settings once only.

To combine the coloured pastas, brush each sheet with egg yolk and layer the yellow and green sheets alternately. Cover the yellow-green pasta block with cling wrap, then weight and refrigerate overnight. Next day, cut the block into 10 mm yellow-green slices and feed through the pasta machine, gradually reducing the setting until the sheets are 1 mm thick. Place the sheets on clean floured tea towels.

To make the ravioli, blend the filling ingredients in the food processor. Brush a pasta sheet with a little beaten egg. Place a spoonful of the filling mixture in the centre and place a pasta sheet on top, gently pressing out any air. Using a fluted cutter cut out the ravioli circles. Gently cook the ravioli, 3 at a time, in boiling salted water for 3 minutes.

To make the truffle sauce, melt the butter in a large saucepan and add the cooked ravioli with the parmesan cheese. Add a little cooking water and sauté the ravioli until you have a creamy sauce. Add the truffle oil and spinach leaves and sauté until the leaves wilt.

Serve the ravioli in warm serving bowls coated with the sauce and the leaves.

roasted scampi with orange crust and tuna with celeriac

serves 6　　*Jacques Reymond* JACQUES REYMOND RESTAURANT MELBOURNE

A well-blended HARMONY of fine seafood FLAVOURED with ASIAN SPICES creating a SOPHISTICATED and UNIQUE dish.

250 g yellow fin tuna
1 celeriac bulb
6 unblemished tatsoi leaves (Japanese chard)
virgin olive oil
2 tablespoons lemon juice
deep-fried celeriac, julienned
300 g fresh egg noodles, cooked and refreshed
30 scampi, shelled, from Western Australia if available
salt and freshly ground black pepper
1/2 bunch spring onions, thinly sliced

LEEK CONFIT
2 young leeks, white part only, cut into 6 cm pieces
1 lemongrass stalk, sliced
1 chilli, deseeded
2 garlic cloves, crushed
2 golden shallots, sliced
olive oil to cover

CARROT TURMERIC
1 tablespoon grated palm sugar
2 teaspoons chopped garlic
1 tablespoon butter
1 tablespoon balsamic vinegar
2 carrots, julienned
5 tablespoons orange juice
2 1/2 tablespoons chicken stock
1 tablespoon olive oil
salt and freshly ground black pepper

CELERIAC WASABI
1 celeriac, peeled
2 tablespoons mayonnaise
1 teaspoon wasabi powder (Japanese horseradish), diluted with 2 teaspoons water
1 drop tabasco sauce
1 tablespoon sour cream
1/2 teaspoon soy sauce

ORANGE CRUST
candied zest 2 oranges

wine suggestion
Dalwhinnie Chardonnay from Pyrenees, Victoria.

To make the leek confit, first preheat the oven to 110°C. Place all the ingredients in a small glass container, cover with baking paper and cook in the preheated oven for 2 hours. Cool. Julienne the leeks and discard the other ingredients.

To make the carrot turmeric, make a blond caramel by melting the palm sugar in a saucepan over a moderate heat. Add the garlic and the butter and deglaze with the vinegar. Add all the other ingredients, season and cook until there are no juices left in the saucepan. Reserve.

To make the celeriac wasabi, julienne the celeriac. Mix the remaining ingredients together and fold in the celeriac. Set aside in a cool place.

To make the orange crust, first preheat the oven to 150°C. Dry the candied zest in the preheated oven for 1–2 hours. When cool, grind it finely in a food mill.

continued page 32

roasted scampi
with orange crust
and tuna with
celeriac

SCAMPI VINAIGRETTE

1 tablespoon pickled
   ginger, chopped
   and blanched
2 tablespoons rice vinegar
3 tablespoons soy sauce
5 tablespoons mirin
   (Japanese rice liquor)
1 tablespoon fish sauce
5 tablespoons almond oil
5 tablespoons olive oil

HONEY DRESSING

1 tablespoon honey
1 teaspoon Szechuan
   pepper
3 tablespoons rice vinegar
2 teaspoons
   chopped garlic
1 tablespoon soy sauce
$2/3$ cup reduced
   chicken stock
5 tablespoons almond oil
5 tablespoons olive oil
juice 1 lime
2 teaspoons diced
   black fungi
2 teaspoons diced sundried
   tomato
2 teaspoons chopped
   chives
2 teaspoons diced
   and blanched zucchini

To make the scampi vinaigrette, mix all the ingredients together and reserve.

To make the honey dressing, caramelise the honey lightly in a saucepan over a moderate heat. When it begins to brown add the Szechuan pepper and deglaze with the vinegar. Reduce the liquid down by one-quarter. Add the garlic, soy sauce and chicken stock and bring to the boil. Add the two oils and the lime juice and remove from the heat. Once it has cooled, mix the fungi, tomato, chives and zucchini into the dressing. Reserve.

To serve the dish, cut the tuna and the raw celeriac into thin strips. Alternate the slices and roll to make up a rose for the centre of each plate. Arrange the tatsoi leaf in the centre of the plates and place the celeriac wasabi on top. Dress the tuna rose with the olive oil and lemon juice and then place on top of the celeriac. Top with the deep-fried celeriac.

Stir-fry the noodles in a wok with the scampi vinaigrette, the carrot turmeric and the leek confit. Place 5 small twirls of noodles around each plate.

Coat the scampi with the orange crust, season with salt and pepper and seal them quickly in a non-stick pan for just 1 minute, until they begin to turn opaque. Place them on top of the noodles and top with the spring onions. Sprinkle the dish with the honey dressing, making sure it is well emulsified first.

chicken salad with spiced peaches

serves 4   *Stephanie Alexander* FOOD WRITER MELBOURNE

This way of SERVING roasted CHICKEN is one of my
FAVOURITES. It has appeared on my menus over and over
again, with SEASONALLY ADJUSTED accompaniments. I choose
chickens from Glenloth, Kangaroo Island or Barossa Chooks.

wine suggestion

I would prefer to drink a
light-bodied, full-flavoured
red with this dish, such as a
grenache shiraz blend, or a
sangiovese. 1997 Crittenden
Sangiovese or 1997 Paul
Conti Grenache Shiraz would
both be delicious.

spiced peaches

The spiced peaches can be
prepared just for the dish
or made much earlier as a
treat through the autumn
and winter. You might even
have some other pickled
or preserved sweet–sour
fruit to create your own
signature dish.

1 x 1.8–2 kg free-range
   chicken
olive oil
60 g unsalted butter
1 tablespoon French
   tarragon, chopped
sea salt
freshly ground
   black pepper
3 thick slices of lemon
2 cloves garlic,
   unpeeled and crushed
4–6 waxy potatoes,
   sliced lengthways into
   5 mm slices
3 tablespoons extra virgin
   olive oil
1/2 cup chicken stock
   or dry white wine
4 handfuls young green
   beans, topped
   and tailed
4 handfuls washed
   and dried salad leaves

SPICED PEACHES
5 cups white wine vinegar
3 1/2 cups sugar
2 teaspoons whole cloves
2 teaspoons black
   peppercorns
1 small hot chilli (optional)
8 ripe medium peaches,
   preferably freestone
   variety

To make the spiced peaches, bring the vinegar, sugar and
spices to the boil, stirring until the sugar has dissolved. Run
a sharp knife around the natural curve of the peach but do not
halve the fruit. Drop the peaches into the simmering syrup
and cook for 5 minutes.

Lift the peaches from the syrup onto a tray using a slotted
spoon. Peel away the skin and discard it. Cut the peach into
pieces and pack into clean, dry jars. Reboil the syrup and allow to
reduce a little. Ladle the hot syrup over the peaches, divide the
spices between the jars (discarding the chilli), seal and leave for
at least a fortnight before using. If you have excess syrup you
could cook a second batch of fruit for your pantry.

To prepare the chicken, remove the chicken legs, leaving
as much skin as possible to protect the breast meat. Reserve
the legs for another dish. Cut the wings off at the first joint.
Cut the chicken either side of the backbone keeping the bony
back and the neck (if present) together with the wingtips to make
a simple chicken stock. Press firmly on the breastbone to flatten
the chicken out. Wipe inside and out with absorbent kitchen
paper. Select a flameproof baking dish a little larger than the
flattened chicken and brush it with a little olive oil.

Preheat the oven to 220°C.

In a small bowl work the butter with the tarragon, salt and
pepper. Carefully loosen the breast skin and slip in two-thirds
of the butter, dividing it between the two sides. Smooth the
skin back into position and work the butter so that it can be seen
as a green-flecked paste through the skin. Distribute the rest
of the butter on the inside of the chicken cavity and finally
smooth your hands over the breast skin. The bird will now look
thoroughly anointed! Squeeze one of the lemon slices over
the bird and place the remaining 2 slices and the garlic in
the baking dish. Place the chicken on top. Place into the
preheated oven for 25 minutes.

continued page 34

main

waxy potatoes

Choose waxy potatoes for this dish, such as kipfler, pink fir apple, bintje or patrone.

While the chicken is cooking, roll the potato slices in the olive oil, spread them on a tray lined with baking paper and place them in the oven on the rack underneath the chicken. Turn the potato slices after 10 minutes. Cook a further 10 minutes. Remove and leave until serving time. (The potatoes will be cooked but not yet completely crisp.)

At the end of 25 minutes, remove the chicken from the oven, place the baking dish over a gas flame and pour in 2 tablespoons of the peach vinegar and the stock. Allow it to bubble and reduce and then cover the chicken loosely with foil and leave to rest in a warm place for 15 minutes, while the beans and potatoes are finished.

Drop the beans into plenty of lightly salted water and cook until just tender. Drain and drop the beans into the baking dish with the chicken and the juices. Return the potatoes to the oven for 5 minutes.

To serve, place a handful of salad leaves on each plate. Cut the breast fillets away from the bone, remove the small underfillet, halve and place half an underfillet on each plate. Carve the breast fillets into thick slices and divide between the plates. Scatter over the green beans and the crisped potatoes. Spoon over the peach and stock juices. Lastly, cut 4 spiced peach halves into bite-sized pieces and divide between the plates.

chicken salad with spiced peaches above and right

teriyaki chicken on roasted pumpkin salad

serves 4   *Sean Macdougall* PARK HYATT JOHANNESBURG

DELICIOUS summer FLAVOURS – Japanese-inspired
GRILLED chicken on a bed of BAKED pumpkin salad.
Pesto sauce and black olive fetta dressing ADD PIQUANCY.

wine suggestion
Leeuwin Estate Rhine
Riesling.

main

4 chicken breasts
1/2 cup pesto sauce
1/2 cup tomato concasse
  (made with 2 tomatoes
  peeled, deseeded and
  finely diced)
fresh coriander sprigs

**BLACK OLIVE FETTA
DRESSING**
80 g fetta cheese
5 tablespoons extra virgin
  olive oil
1/2 cup pitted and
  quartered kalamata olives
1 teaspoon finely chopped
  fresh rosemary
1 teaspoon finely chopped
  and seeded chillies
salt and freshly ground
  black pepper

PUMPKIN SALAD
3 cups diced pumpkin
  (1 cm cubes)
salt and freshly ground
  black pepper
2 tablespoons olive oil
1 cup peeled, deseeded
  and julienned tomatoes
1/4 cup freshly chopped
  parsley

TERIYAKI SAUCE
1/2 cup Japanese soy sauce
1/2 cup sake
  (Japanese rice wine)
1/2 cup mirin
  (Japanese rice liquor)
1/2 cup sugar

To make the black olive fetta dressing, crumble the fetta cheese and mix with the olive oil, olives and rosemary. Season with the chillies, salt and pepper and reserve.

Preheat the oven to 200°C.

To make the pumpkin salad, season the pumpkin with salt and pepper and sauté in the olive oil in a hot frying pan. When it begins to colour bake it in the preheated oven for 10 minutes, until tender. Remove from the oven and cool. Place in a bowl and mix with the tomato, parsley and half the black olive fetta dressing.

Make the teriyaki sauce by mixing the soy sauce, sake and mirin together. Put in a small saucepan, add the sugar and heat. As soon as the sugar is dissolved, remove from the heat and cool. Marinate the chicken breasts in this for 30 minutes.

Grill the chicken breasts on a preheated grill, brushing with teriyaki sauce when turning. They should take 15 minutes to cook on each side.

To serve, place the pumpkin salad in the centre of each plate with a chicken breast on top. Drizzle a little pesto sauce around each plate along with the remainder of the black olive fetta dressing and the tomato concasse. Garnish with fresh coriander sprigs.

sugar cane prawn sticks with sweet chilli lemon myrtle dipping sauce

serves 4   *Craig Squire* RED OCHRE GRILL CAIRNS

This one is a WINNER for the summer BARBECUE. Vietnamese in origin, but Australian to the core! It is GREAT PARTY FOOD and FUN to EAT – don't forget to suck all the JUICE from the sugar cane as well. The ART of this dish is in the packing of the prawn mixture on the sugar cane sticks.

8 sugar cane sticks
olive oil
2 cups steamed
    jasmine rice, warm
2 spring onions,
    sliced diagonally
1 red capsicum,
    sliced finely and
    soaked in water
black sesame seeds
sprigs fresh coriander
    leaves, chopped

PRAWN MIXTURE
600 g prawn meat,
    from North Queensland
    if available
1 teaspoon sambal oelek
1¹/2 tablespoons
    sesame oil
2 spring onions, chopped
1 tablespoon salt
    and freshly ground
    black pepper
¹/2 cup fresh coriander,
    chopped
2 egg whites

DIPPING SAUCE
4 cups water
1 cup sugar
³/4 cup rice wine vinegar
5 tablespoons fish sauce
2 large green chillies,
    sliced finely
2 tablespoons ginger,
    julienned
1 tablespoon soy sauce
25 fresh lemon myrtle
    leaves, julienned
2 tablespoons cornflour

To prepare the sugar cane sticks, wash the cane sticks and then cut them into 15–20 cm lengths. Divide each length into 4 sticks.

To make the prawn mixture, purée all the ingredients in a food processor to bind them together coarsely. Oil your better hand, hold the cut sugar cane in the other, pick up a handful of prawn mixture and wrap it onto the cane. Be careful not to get too much oil in with the mixture. Smooth the prawn mixture to neaten it.

To make the dipping sauce, simmer all the ingredients except for the cornflour for 10 minutes. Thicken slightly with the cornflour, which has been mixed first with a little cold water.

Barbecue the prawn sticks on a very hot flat plate of a barbecue or grill until just cooked, that is, the meat is turning opaque.

To serve, place the prawn sticks on the steamed jasmine rice with a little of the sweet chilli lemon myrtle dipping sauce. Garnish with spring onions, red capsicum strips, sesame seeds and chopped coriander.

sweet chilli lemon myrtle dipping sauce

The dipping sauce recipe here is for a large amount, because it is a great sauce to have on hand to eat with any seafood. It will keep in the refrigerator for months.

wine suggestion
Australian sparkling.

main

steamed Murray cod served with a nage of oyster mushrooms, lime and broad beans

serves 4   *Guillaume Brahimi* QUAY RESTAURANT SYDNEY

Our FINEST freshwater fish is served À LA NAGE in this SIMPLE SUMMER DISH, that is, it is served in an AROMATIC COURT BOUILLON with oyster mushrooms and broad beans.

wine suggestion
1998 Gembrook Hill
Sauvignon Blanc, Yarra Valley.

250 g broad beans,
  removed from pod
4 x 200 g Murray cod
  fillets
1 bunch fresh dill,
  picked over
1 bunch fresh chervil,
  picked over
knob butter
250 g oyster mushrooms,
  wiped clean

NAGE
2 large onions
2 large carrots
4 cups white wine
zest 1 orange
zest 1 lime
1 star anise
20 coriander seeds
20 white peppercorns

To make the nage, peel and slice the onions and carrots. Bring the wine to the boil in a saucepan over a medium heat and add the onion, carrots, orange and lime zest, star anise, coriander and pepper. Boil for 5 minutes, then pass through a fine sieve and reserve. Heat up just before serving.

Peel the broad beans and cook them in boiling water for 5 minutes. Immerse immediately in iced water to refresh. Steam the Murray cod fillets in a steamer for 6 minutes. Chop the dill and chervil.

To serve, whisk the butter into the nage, then add the herbs, broad beans and oyster mushrooms. Distribute the nage and vegetables in 4 shallow soup bowls and place a Murray cod fillet on top of each and serve immediately.

main

pan-fried King George whiting with orange and fennel confit

serves 4   *Simon Fenwick* THE SUGAR CLUB LONDON

When choosing fish the FRESHNESS and QUALITY of the flesh is important. Look for a CLEAR eye and GOOD COLOUR — in this case white FIRM FLESH. Ask your FISHMONGER to fillet and skin the fish.

wine suggestion

1998 Mt Langi Ghiran Riesling or 1998 Katnook Sauvignon Blanc.

1 knob clarified butter
2 tablespoons virgin olive oil
4 King George whiting fillets
salt and freshly ground black pepper
1 orange or blood orange, segmented and with pith removed
extra virgin olive oil

FENNEL CONFIT
2 1/2 tablespoons peanut oil
2 1/2 tablespoons olive oil
1 onion, cut into 2 cm dice
2 fennel bulbs, cut into 2 cm dice
2 garlic cloves, finely chopped
2 dried bay leaves
1/2 teaspoon fennel seeds
5 tablespoons freshly squeezed orange juice
3 tablespoons Pernod
2 tablespoons red wine vinegar, Forum Cabernet Sauvignon if available
1 teaspoon fresh dill, chopped
1/2 teaspoon fresh thyme, chopped
2 tablespoons chopped fresh parsley
6 anchovies, chopped, Ortiz if available

To make the fennel confit, gently heat the oils in a saucepan and add the onion and fennel, cooking gently over a low to moderate heat to keep translucent. Once these are soft, add the garlic and gently cook for 30 minutes, keeping the heat low.

While the fennel and onion mix is cooking, roast the bay leaves and fennel seeds in a dry frying pan until fragrant, then grind to a powder.

In a separate saucepan, reduce the orange juice by half. Add the orange juice, Pernod and vinegar to the fennel and onion mix, and continue to cook slowly for 15 minutes, or until the confit becomes thicker. Finally, add the dill, thyme, parsley, the roasted spices and the chopped anchovies. Cook for another 5 minutes only.

To cook the fish, gently heat the clarified butter and virgin olive oil in a frying pan. Season the fish with salt and pepper. Pan-fry the fillets until golden brown.

To serve, spoon the confit mixture onto 4 warm plates, along with a couple of orange segments, and place the cooked fish on top. Drizzle with a little extra virgin olive oil.

main

Tasmanian lobster and
potato layers with basil sauce

serves 4   *Timothy Fisher and Lucio Galletto* LUCIO'S RESTAURANT SYDNEY

The NATURALLY SWEET FLAVOURS of lobster and basil

go extremely well together and the DIFFERENT COOKING

METHOD of the legs gives a WONDERFUL red COLOUR

to the dish.

main

wine suggestion
Cape Mentelle Semillon
Sauvignon from the Margaret
River, Western Australia.

1 x 700 g live lobster,
  Tasmanian if available
2 large desirée potatoes
olive oil
salt and freshly ground
  black pepper

BASIL SAUCE
1 bunch fresh basil,
  picked over
splash sherry vinegar
6 tablespoons extra
  virgin olive oil
salt and freshly ground
  black pepper

Preheat the oven to 200°C.

To prepare the lobster, numb the lobster in the freezer
for about 30 minutes. Remove it and slice through the head
with one very fast action. Remove the head and legs, discarding
the head. Cook the legs in boiling salted water for 3 minutes.
With a small meat mallet, crack the shells to extract the meat.
Using a sharp pair of lobster scissors, cut the shell from the
lobster tail. Divide the meat into 12 even slices and set aside with
the leg meat.

To prepare the potatoes, peel and trim them into a square
shape then slice thinly, to make at least 16 slices. Boil the slices
in salted water for about 5 minutes. While the potatoes are
cooking, make the basil sauce.

To make the basil sauce, place the basil, vinegar, olive oil, salt
and pepper in a blender and pulse until the basil sauce is smooth.

Heat some olive oil in a frying pan over a medium heat,
season the slices of lobster with salt and pepper and sauté for
2 minutes on each side. Remove from the pan and leave to rest
while you organise the 4 serving plates.

To serve, arrange a slice of potato in the centre of each plate,
then a piece of cooked lobster. Repeat layering, finishing with
a potato slice. Top with the cooked lobster legs and heat through
in the oven for 2 minutes. Serve with a drizzle of basil sauce.

roast Murray cod with spinach, sultana and pinenuts

serves 6   *Stefano Manfredi* BEL MONDO SYDNEY

The SUBTLE FLAVOUR and TEXTURE of our finest freshwater fish is ENHANCED by the spinach, sultana and pinenut accompaniment. A QUICKLY MADE dish for a very FRESH fish.

wine suggestion
Petaluma Tiers Chardonnay.

main

Murray cod

The Murray cod is Australia's finest freshwater fish. It is classed as a giant freshwater perch and can grow to over 100 kg. It is found in the Murray–Darling river system of eastern Australia and is considered an endangered species. Bruce Malcolm farms Murray cod at a place called Grong Grong near Wagga in western New South Wales. The fish is delivered to our kitchen in wonderful condition at 2.5–3.5 kg per fish. At this weight the fish are 3–4 years old.

olive oil
1 x 1.2 kg Murray cod
   fillet, skin on and cut
   into pieces, about
   6 x 180 g
4 tablespoons black
   olive paste
150 g spinach,
   cleaned and trimmed
50 g butter
$1/4$ cup finely grated
   parmesan cheese
$1/4$ cup toasted pinenuts
$1/4$ cup sultanas
salt and freshly ground
   black pepper

To cook the cod, heat some olive oil in a frying pan and sear the cod, skin side down. Place in a hot oven for about 8–10 minutes. The cod should still be opaque in the middle. Spread a little of the olive paste thinly on the skin side of the cod, then rest in a warm place.

To serve, blanch the spinach in boiling water for about 1 minute. Drain well and place in a large warm bowl. Quickly throw the butter, parmesan cheese, pinenuts and sultanas onto the spinach while it is at its hottest. Mix well, season and serve immediately on warm serving plates next to the cod.

roasted marron from Parkerville
with citrus sauce

serves 4   *Alain Fabrègues* THE LOOSE BOX RESTAURANT MUNDARING

The recipe is SIMPLE so as not to disturb the FINE FLAVOURS and texture of this SPLENDID NATIVE CRUSTACEAN. After all, it is the role of GOOD COOKS to take a common product and through skill give it a certain NOBILITY.

wine suggestion

Leeuwin Estate Art Series Sauvignon Blanc 1998, because it is very light, fresh and crisp, with delicate acid and sugar balance that complements the sweet marron flesh and the citrus in the sauce.

marron

A few kilometres from my restaurant is the peaceful village of Parkerville and nestled in a pear orchard is a marron farm that Harry Cassian has been farming for 20 years. He gives us his best specimens, and they are of exceptional quality. I have created this recipe to honour these marrons. With such a noble product to begin with, the cook should be content to marry flavours that most complement it without tinkering.

4 x 250 g live marron,
  from Parkerville,
  if available
16 stringless green beans
8 baby carrots
1 tablespoon olive oil
200 g fresh fettuccine
knob butter
salt and freshly ground
  black pepper
sprigs fresh chervil or dill
chives, finely sliced

CITRUS SAUCE
1 lemon
1/2 grapefruit
1 orange
100 ml vegetable stock
100 g butter, cold and
  diced, plus extra
salt and freshly ground
  black pepper

Preheat the oven to 210°C.

To prepare the marron, immerse them in a large saucepan of boiling salted water for 1 1/2 minutes. Remove and refresh in iced water. Remove the shell and the spinal cord from the flesh. Crack the claws and remove the flesh, being very careful not to break the flesh. Wash and clean the heads carefully and shorten them by trimming with sharp kitchen scissors. Put the heads aside for garnishing the dish.

To make the citrus sauce, segment the lemon, grapefruit and orange, removing all the pips and white pith. Bring the vegetable stock to the boil and add the citrus segments. Cook for 5 minutes. Place in a blender or food processor and blend at high speed. Add the cold diced butter and blend into a smooth sauce. Check the seasoning and add salt and pepper to taste. Reserve in a warm place. Be careful that the sauce does not get hot (above 55°C), otherwise it will separate.

Top and tail the stringless green beans. Blanch in boiling salted water and refresh in iced water. Peel the baby carrots, blanch in boiling salted water and refresh in iced water. Season the marron with salt and pepper. Heat a frying pan over a high heat and add the olive oil. When hot, quickly seal the marron tails. Place them in the oven for 5 minutes. Remove from the oven and let them rest for 4 minutes in a warm place.

Cook the fresh fettuccine in boiling salted water for about 1 1/2 minutes, or until al dente. Drain well and toss with a knob of butter, a pinch of salt and a twist of pepper. Heat the beans and baby carrots in 2 tablespoons of boiling water and a little fresh butter.

To serve, roll some fettuccine onto a long toasting fork and then place the fettuccine in the centre of a warm plate. With a sharp, heavy knife slice the marron tail into 4 pieces lengthways. Arrange the slices on top of the bed of fettuccine, keeping the shape of the tail. Place the carrots and beans decoratively on either side of the marron tail. Put the head at the top of the plate and the claws at the bottom. Emulsify the sauce with a handheld blender and spoon it over the tail and fettuccine. Garnish with the chervil or dill and chives. Serve immediately.

dessert

watermelon, honeydew melon and rockmelon granitas

serves 6   *Janni Kyritsis* MG GARAGE RESTAURANT SYDNEY

These REFRESHING summer desserts require some
INITIATIVE from the cook! Serve these DELICIOUS and
COLOURFUL granitas with buttery dessert biscuits.

wine suggestion
1997 Mt Horrocks Cordon
Cut Riesling, Clare Valley.

1/2 small watermelon
1 small honeydew melon
2 knobs preserved ginger
juice 1 lemon
1/2 rockmelon
kirsch

SUGAR SYRUP
1 cup sugar
1 cup water

To make the sugar syrup, place the sugar and water in a saucepan and bring to the boil. Remove from the heat and cool.

Scoop the flesh out of the watermelon and squeeze it through a fine sieve.

Scoop out the flesh from the honeydew melon and blend in food processor with some ginger to taste. Pass the mixture through a fine sieve. Adjust the flavour to taste with lemon juice and sugar syrup.

Scoop the flesh from the rockmelon and blend, then pass it through a fine sieve. Stir in some kirsch, lemon juice and sugar syrup to taste.

Put the 3 purées in 3 separate trays and freeze. Take them from the freezer occasionally and stir the setting ice with a fork to create the granita flakes. Depending on your freezer, they should freeze in 3–4 hours.

Serve in layers in a martini glass or any other glass of your choice. About 2 cups each of melon juice should be plenty for 6 people.

dessert

cherries Santa Lucia with lemongrass sorbetto and vanilla gelato

serves 4   *Stefano Manfredi* BEL MONDO SYDNEY

This DELICIOUS summer dessert needs to be started at least the day before, then all you have to do on the day is assemble. The SANTA LUCIA crumbs are actually a TRADITIONAL POLENTA SHORTBREAD called 'sbrisolona' from my native Lombardy – usually served on the FEAST of Santa Lucia.

wine suggestion

Bel mondo Moscato 1999 made from fruit grown for us at Collina del Re in north-east Victoria.

cherries

My preferred cherries for this dessert are dark Rons from Tasmania that come late in the summer season. The cool climate there means that ripening occurs slowly but the flavours develop with more intensity.

VANILLA GELATO
2/3 cup sugar
8 egg yolks
1 vanilla bean,
   sliced lengthways
4 cups cream

LEMONGRASS SORBETTO
4 stalks lemongrass,
   finely chopped
4 cups sugar syrup
   (2 cups sugar dissolved
   in 2 cups water)
4 cups lemon juice

SANTA LUCIA CRUMBS
1 cup plain flour
3/4 cup fine polenta flour
1/3 cup sugar
3/4 cup ground
   almond meal
grated zest 1 lemon
80 g butter, melted
5 tablespoons duck fat
   or goose fat, melted
1 teaspoon vanilla essence
2 tablespoons grappa

To make the vanilla gelato, beat the sugar and egg yolks together in a bowl until they are pale. Scrape the vanilla seeds into the cream then heat the cream almost to the boil, but be careful not to boil. Remove from the heat and whisk in the egg and sugar mixture. Place on a low heat and stir continuously with a wooden spoon until the mixture thickens and coats the spoon. Cool completely before freezing in an ice cream maker according to the manufacturer's instructions.

To make the lemongrass sorbetto, steep the lemongrass in the hot sugar syrup and allow to cool and stand for 12 hours in the refrigerator. Add the lemon juice, strain the lemongrass then freeze in an ice cream maker according to the manufacturer's instructions.

To make the Santa Lucia crumbs, first preheat the oven to 150°C. Sift the flour into a large bowl and mix all the dry ingredients together. Add the remaining crumb ingredients and mix thoroughly by rubbing the mixture between palms. Lay the crumbs on flat baking trays and bake for 40 minutes in the oven, then lower the temperature to 80°C for 2–3 hours, until the crumbs have firmed and dried. Once cool they are ready to use.

dessert

CHERRIES

4 cups dry red wine

1 tablespoon honey

1 stick cinnamon

pinch each cloves,
  peppercorns and
  star anise

1 vanilla bean,
  sliced in half

zest and juice 1 lemon
  and 1 orange

500 g cherries, pitted

To cook the cherries, place all the ingredients except the cherries in a saucepan and reduce the liquid by about half over a simmering heat. Strain all the spices from the liquid, add the cherries, then bring it back to the boil. Remove the cherries from the liquid, allow liquid to cool, then store the cherries in the juice.

To serve, decoratively spoon some cherries and their liquid on each plate, sprinkle Santa Lucia crumbs over, then some vanilla gelato, top with lemongrass sorbetto and finally sprinkle with more crumbs.

cherries Santa
Lucia with
lemongrass
sorbetto and
vanilla gelato

summer pudding

It's always summer on HAMILTON ISLAND, and one of the most POPULAR desserts in my restaurant is this LIGHT and REFRESHING dish.

wine suggestion
Goundrey Boytritis Riesling.

berries

I believe that Australian produce is the best in the world – the freshest array of strawberries, blackberries, raspberries and blueberries are sourced from local markets or from Brisbane and then air-freighted to the island.

50 g raspberries,
   puréed and strained
2 tablespoons
   Grand Marnier
1 punnet blueberries,
   washed and dried
1 punnet strawberries,
   washed and dried
1 punnet raspberries,
   washed and dried
1 punnet blackberries,
   washed and dried
few drops lemon juice
1/2 cup thick cream
   such as King Island

FRENCH TOAST
6 eggs
1 teaspoon caster sugar
pinch ground cinnamon
12 slices fresh baguette

SUGAR SYRUP
1/2 cup water
1/2 cup sugar

To make the egg wash for the French Toast, lightly mix the eggs and flavour with the caster sugar and cinnamon.

Soak the bread in the egg wash. Remove the bread from the egg wash and allow to drain a little. Place 2 slices of bread in a preheated frying pan over a medium heat and cook until they are golden brown. Set aside and keep warm.

To make the sugar syrup, place the water and sugar in a saucepan over a medium heat and bring to the boil. Add the puréed raspberries and the Grand Marnier, stir, then add all the berries. Toss for 20 seconds to heat through. Add a little lemon juice to dilute the sweet taste. Remove from heat.

To serve, place 2 slices of toast on each warmed serving plate and pour the berries on top. Finish with a dollop of cream on the side.

dessert

autumn

autumn

AUTUMN is a season

I await with a PASSION.

Time for GAME and

MUSHROOMS. Not as

popular as they used to

be, but I am OPTIMISTIC

that today's young

hamburger eaters will turn

in time to recognising the

COMPLEX and DEEP

FLAVOURS of an autumn

HARE or PHEASANT.

—*Tony Bilson*

At Bilson's Restaurant at Circular Quay we had the privilege of cooking for Paul Bocuse. He asked to see the kitchen and I introduced him to my brigade. 'The Emperor', as he is known, asked to see the coolroom and when shown was amazed to see fifteen brace of pheasant hanging in their feathers – each of the apprentices was required to pluck three a day.

When I was a child growing up in Colac we would go mushrooming, and had great fun finding the large field mushrooms in the grassy paddocks. We never thought of looking for other wild mushrooms in the forest. In fact the first experience I had of finding morels was at Yalumba winery in Angaston. Peter Wall, then chief winemaker, showed me the chardonnay cuttings they were propagating. The cuttings were struck in milk cartons and had pine chips as a mulch. From the mulch were growing morels. Things have changed since then, and in autumn the markets have all sorts of wonderful mushrooms.

Alain Fabrègues searches out the mushrooms himself. His mushroom terrine captures the essence of autumn in colour, smell and taste. Maggie Beer is famous for her

development of local produce. Here she uses her local yabbies and wild boletus to create a dish that is a celebration of both season and locality. Graeme Phillips' dish of Tasmanian highland venison on red wine and wild mushroom risotto brings together all that is special about autumn.

The other side of autumn produce is the late-picked fruits and berries, especially ripe, sweet figs and quinces. Hermann Schneider's recipe for fresh figs teams the finest of the seasonal fruits with a wonderful late-picked riesling.

An ode to autumn indeed.

—*Tony Bilson*

Our restaurant is situated in the heart of Mundaring, on the edge of the state pine forest. Each autumn we go into the forest to collect mushrooms. It is the time of year when the shadows stretch forever in the pine forest, the pale sun has difficulty penetrating the undergrowth and the mist stays stagnant until late in the morning.

—*Alain Fabrègues*

Frosty mornings. Still, crisp, sunny days. Autumn colours. The smell of winter, hiding. From the lakes, trout move slowly up the small streams to spawn. Fallow deer move down from the hills closer to winter feed, the does heavy with next season's fawns. Wild mushrooms appear in secret places to be picked by those that know. Pheasants and wild ducks are in season.

Apples and pears are stored away. Oysters are approaching their winter best. Late riesling grapes hang on the vines to botrytise in the autumn mist. Home fires are lit. And in restaurants, slow braises, rich quince desserts, pickled walnuts, goose and duck appear on the menu. But, most of all for me, a Tasmanian autumn is the season for game.

—Graeme Phillips

The debate on whether there is an Australian cuisine has long ceased. We are now celebrating not only our much-heralded cuisine, but we are exposing its regional quirks.

—Geoff Lindsay

I love the international variety of food such as the Asian and European products which we have grown locally in Australia for years. It makes it possible to create truly contemporary dishes without having to call them fusion or words to that effect. They are local produce now, and extremely good quality produce at that. The result is contemporary Australian cuisine.

—David Laris

I believe that Australian regionalism will become more apparent in the next 8–10 years. Areas already famous for their food products such as the Barossa with its game and baby chickens, Horsham for olive oil and the Yarra Valley for salmon, kid and game will become even better known. Certain dishes will become mainstays, while we continue to grow and mature with our multicultural influences. To keep ahead of this growth and to lead the world with our cuisine we will have to change constantly. This will make exciting times for both chefs and patrons.

—Gary Cooper

Ever since migrating to Australia and being given the chance to work with various food products from the far north to Tasmania and the islands in Bass Strait, I am convinced that Australia is an environment which naturally has a tendency to evolve its own standards and style of foods.

—Warren Pearson

an autumn menu

smoked salmon salad with

celeriac, cucumber, witlof

and ocean trout caviar

◊

tasmanian highland venison

on red wine and

wild mushroom risotto

◊

fresh figs poached in a

citrus syrup with mascarpone

ice parfait

wine suggestions

1999 Meerea Park

Semillon Sauvignon Blanc

◊

1994 Rotherhythe or

1990 Morningside Pinot Noir

◊

Essency Late Picked Riesling

or a pinot noir champagne

Pages 60–61: Long Gully Estate Vineyard.

hot pot of ahi-flavoured tuna steak with somen noodles, jalapeño, kimchi and shiitake

serves 4   *James Doherty* INFLIGHT CHEF ANSETT INTERNATIONAL

This TUNA dish, which we offer on our Ansett aircraft, is one of our HEALTHY LIGHT MEALS that incorporates the freshest of Australian SEAFOOD and Asian VEGETABLES.

wine suggestion
Eileen Hardy Chardonnay 1995. This splendid wine has a rich and complex bouquet with tangy fruit and spicy French oak.

360 g tuna steak, cut into a long roll, Southern Blue Fin if available
2 tablespoons olive oil
8 halves baby bok choy, steamed
20 thin slices jalapeño chillies
60 g kimchi (Korean pickled cabbage)
160 g somen noodles, cooked
80 g baby carrots, sliced diagonally, blanched
50 g shiitake mushrooms, steamed and sliced
4 3/4 cups strong beef stock, boiling

AHI SEASONING
1/4 teaspoon cayenne pepper
2 1/2 teaspoons ground coriander
2 tablespoons cracked peppercorns
1 1/2 tablespoons ground cumin
2 tablespoons sesame seeds
2 1/2 tablespoons mustard seeds
1 tablespoon fresh thyme leaves, chopped

To make the ahi seasoning, mix all the ingredients together and store in an airtight container. It can be kept in the refrigerator for 3 days.

To cook the tuna, roll it in the ahi herbs. Place the olive oil in a frying pan and, over a high heat, sear the tuna on all sides. Remove from the heat and cut into 4 portions.

To serve, place all the remaining ingredients except the stock and tuna in the bottom of 4 warmed deep bowls. Pour over the boiling stock and place a seared piece of tuna on top for each bowl.

smoked salmon salad with celeriac, cucumber, witlof and ocean trout caviar

serves 6–8

Peter Doyle CICADA SYDNEY

I like to make this SIMPLE SALAD in autumn when all the ingredients are at their best – especially the OCEAN TROUT CAVIAR. Toasted brioche COMPLEMENTS the salad perfectly.

wine suggestion
1999 Meerea Park
Semillon Sauvignon Blanc,
Hunter Valley.

beer suggestion
Carlton Premium Dry.

2 tablespoons lemon juice
¾ cup extra virgin
  olive oil
sea salt and freshly
  ground black pepper
2 bulbs witlof
2 cups mache
1 cup curly endive
8 tablespoons celeriac,
  julienned
8 tablespoons cucumber,
  julienned
4 tablespoons radish,
  julienned
2 tablespoons chopped
  chives
sea salt and freshly
  ground black pepper
24 slices smoked salmon,
  from Tasmania if
  available
8 tablespoons mayonnaise
2 tablespoons ocean trout
  caviar, from Macquarie
  Harbour if available

To make the lemon vinaigrette, mix together the lemon juice and olive oil with a little salt and pepper.

To compose the salad, place some witlof leaves in the centre of each serving plate. Toss the mache and curly endive in a bowl with a little of the lemon vinaigrette and place some on top of the witlof.

To make the julienne mixture, place the celeriac, cucumber, radish and chives in a bowl and season with a little salt and pepper. Toss with some of the lemon vinaigrette.

Place a slice of salmon on top of the salad on the plate and top with a little of the julienne mixture. Drizzle a little mayonnaise over the vegetables. Repeat with the mache and endive, salmon and julienne mixture, then repeat again.

Finish with a little smoked salmon on top and place a teaspoon of ocean trout caviar on the salmon. Spoon little dabs of mayonnaise around the salad and add some lemon vinaigrette between the mayonnaise dabs. Serve immediately.

hot spiced mussels with coconut and coriander

serves 4   *Mark Haynes* HOTEL LINDRUM MELBOURNE

This dish reflects some of the ASIAN INFLUENCES apparent in AUSTRALIAN CUISINE today. The mussels from Western Port Bay, Victoria, have been chosen for their HIGH QUALITY and FULLNESS OF FLAVOUR.

wine suggestion
Giants Creek Chardonnay,
1998 Rosemount wines.

2 kg small black mussels,
  from Western Port Bay,
  if available
1/2 cup freshly chopped
  coriander, plus extra
  sprigs
fresh red and green
  chillies, sliced

COCONUT SAUCE
5 garlic cloves
2 knobs fresh ginger,
  peeled and chopped
1 cup water
1 cup chopped onions
1/2 teaspoon
  vegetable oil
1/2 teaspoon ground
  turmeric
1/2 teaspoon ground cumin
2 hot chillies, finely
  chopped
1/2 block coconut cream,
  grated or 1 cup
  coconut milk

To make the coconut sauce, blend the garlic, ginger and half a cup of water in a food processor until smooth. Cook the onion gently in the vegetable oil in a large pan over a medium heat until transparent. Add the turmeric, cumin and chillies and cook for a few minutes until the mixture forms a paste. Add the garlic and ginger mixture and the remaining half cup of water. Bring to the boil then reduce to a simmer and cook until the sauce thickens. Add the coconut and dissolve. Blend the sauce in a food processor, then pass it through a sieve.

To cook the mussels, place them in a large saucepan and add the coconut sauce. Place a lid on the pan and put it over a high heat. Cook for 5–6 minutes, until the mussels are open. Remove from the heat immediately and serve in large pasta bowls. Garnish with the chopped coriander, coriander sprigs and red and green chillies.

brodetto di mare con zafferano zucchini e fregola

serves 4   *Simon Humble* SCUSA MI RISTORANTE MELBOURNE

A selection of AUSTRALIAN SEAFOOD in a SAFFRON and ZUCCHINI broth with SARDINIAN PASTA.

wine suggestion
1998 Howard Park Riesling.

seafood

I like to use the finest of Australia's wonderful seafood. In this dish the octopus and the fish are local to Melbourne, the mussels are from Flinders in Victoria, the prawns are from Ocean King in Queensland and the pippies are from Yamba, in New South Wales.

fregola

Fregola means crumbs in Italian – it is actually pasta that looks like breadcrumbs, made from fine semolina flour.

1 garlic clove, crushed
1 fresh red chilli
2 tablespoons extra virgin olive oil, Toscana if available
12 black-shelled mussels, shells scrubbed
12 pippies, shells scrubbed
4 small red mullet, cleaned
4 baby octopus, cleaned
12 prawns, shelled and deveined
sea salt and freshly ground black pepper
1/2 teaspoon saffron threads, crushed
5 cups fish stock, boiling
30 g Sardinian fregola
2 zucchini, grated
extra virgin olive oil

To make the broth, lightly sauté the garlic and chilli in the olive oil in a large, heavy-based saucepan. Add all the seafood and season with salt and pepper. Add the crushed saffron, fish stock and fregola and simmer gently until the seafood is cooked, about 3–4 minutes. Stir in the grated zucchini at the last minute. Drizzle with the extra virgin olive oil.

terrine of cèpes and other mushrooms from the Mundaring State Forest

serves 14   *Alain Fabrègues* THE LOOSE BOX RESTAURANT MUNDARING

Each autumn we go into the FOREST to collect our own MUSHROOMS. We use our own dried mushrooms to make the sauce for this TERRINE.

wine suggestion
Moss Wood Pinot Noir 1996, because it is lightly spiced and earthy without a big berry hit.

mushrooms

… I found three types of mushrooms in the forest nearby, all from the boletus family – in France we call them pine cèpes. They have a great texture and a pleasant flavour. I combine these with common field mushrooms and oyster mushrooms, which are easily found in shops.

TERRINE
1 onion, chopped
2 stems fresh flat-leafed parsley
5 teaspoons olive oil, plus extra
25 g butter
400 g mixed mushrooms
2 cups cream
$1^{1}/_{3}$ cups chicken stock
1 cup egg whites
2 egg yolks
salt and freshly ground black pepper
800 g cèpes
1 handful garlic cloves, coarsely chopped
1 handful chopped fresh flat-leafed parsley

SAUCE
1 handful dried cèpes, soaked and patted dry
1 handful dried morels, soaked and patted dry
2 cups cream
salt and freshly ground black pepper

2 cups whipped cream

Preheat the oven to 170°C.

To prepare the mushroom mix, sauté the onion and parsley in the olive oil and butter, then add the mushrooms. Cook slowly on a low heat, covered, for 15 minutes, then add the cream and a little of the chicken stock – enough to cover the mushrooms. Cook for 15 minutes then sieve and save the liquid.

In the food processor, combine the mushroom cream mixture with the egg whites, then add the egg yolks and the cooking liquid from the mushrooms. Season with salt and pepper.

Slice the cèpes, sauté them in olive oil over a medium heat and season with salt, pepper, the garlic and the parsley. Cook until wilted. Reserve.

To set the terrine, line the terrine mould with silicone paper. Make a layer of cèpes, then a layer of mushroom cream mixture and continue the process to the top of the terrine. Cover the terrine with silicone paper, then foil, and place in a water bath (a deep baking tray that has 2 cm water brought to a simmer in it). Cook in the oven for 30 minutes. When the terrine is cooked, all the liquid will have set. Cool and store in the refrigerator overnight.

To make the sauce, finely chop the cèpes and morels and put them into a small saucepan with the cream. Let it reduce until it has thickened to a sauce consistency. Season with salt and pepper.

To serve, cut the terrine into slices 2 cm thick. Put a slice in a bowl or deep entrée plate, cover with cling wrap and heat for 1 minute in the microwave or cover with silicone paper or foil and heat for 4 minutes in an oven preheated to 170°C. Fold the whipped cream into the sauce and pour over the terrine slices, then immediately put the dishes under a preheated grill for a couple of minutes until it has turned a golden colour. If you have a cloche to put over the dish until it arrives at the table the perfume when the cloche is removed will fill the dining room and increase everyone's appetite and delight.

goat's cheese ravioli with pickled spiced beetroot

serves 6   *Christine Manfield* THE PARAMOUNT RESTAURANT SYDNEY

HEADY, AROMATIC FLAVOURS work harmoniously together here to produce a perfect balance of TASTE AND TEXTURE. A wonderful start to a WINTER MENU.

wine suggestion
A cool climate pinot noir from Victoria or Tasmania.

goat's cheese
Use Kervella cheese from Western Australia or Meredith Farm in Victoria (if available) for this recipe.

175 g fresh goat's cheese
2 tablespoons shredded
  basil leaves
1 tablespoon finely diced
  fennel bulb
salt and freshly ground
  black pepper
24 fresh pasta rounds,
  6 cm in diameter
egg wash made from
  1 beaten egg yolk
18 small beetroot leaves
  washed and trimmed
a few dandelion leaves,
  washed and trimmed
2 teaspoons
  white truffle oil
extra freshly ground black
  pepper

PICKLED SPICED BEETROOT*
6 large beetroot
1 1/3 cups malt vinegar
1/3 cup dark brown sugar
3 whole cloves
2 teaspoons minced
  fresh ginger
3 garlic cloves, minced
2 red bird's eye chillies,
  minced
1/4 teaspoon fennel seeds,
  roasted and ground
10 black peppercorns,
  cracked
1 teaspoon sea salt

To prepare the spiced beetroot, cook the beetroot whole in a large pot of boiling water until soft. Peel them and refresh in cold water, then coarsely grate them into a large bowl.

Put the remaining ingredients into a saucepan and bring to the boil. Simmer for 45 minutes or until the liquid has reduced by one-third its volume. Pour the hot liquid over the grated beetroot and allow to cool. Serve slightly warmed for this recipe.

To assemble the ravioli, mix the goat's cheese, basil and fennel in a bowl and season to taste with salt and pepper. Brush 8 pasta rounds with egg wash and spoon the filling onto the centres of each round. Firmly press the remaining pasta rounds over the filling to enclose and form the ravioli. Lay on a floured tray until ready to cook.

Bring a large pot of water to a rolling boil and add the ravioli, one by one, to prevent sticking. Cook for 2 minutes, then remove carefully with a slotted spoon and reserve in a warm place. Arrange the spiced beetroot on serving plates, scatter a few beetroot leaves and dandelion leaves over and sit the ravioli on top of the leaves. Drizzle over the white truffle oil and a little freshly ground black pepper and serve immediately.

* From *Spice* by Christine Manfield, published by Penguin Books, 1999. The recipe makes 500 ml and the leftovers can be kept in the refrigerator for up to 3 months.

peppered carpaccio of veal, chargrilled baby leeks, fig salad, balsamic vinegar and herb oil

serves 4

Grant MacPherson BELLAGIO RESORT LAS VEGAS

I love using the FINE FRUITS and beautiful GRAIN-FED MEAT that are PRODUCED IN AUSTRALIA. This dish needs to be started the day before serving.

main

8 baby leeks
  or spring onions
salt and freshly ground
  black pepper
4 black figs
rock salt
1 cup red grapes, seared
  in a hot frying pan
4 tablespoons aged
  balsamic vinegar
4 cups mesclun
extra salt and freshly
  ground black pepper

CARPACCIO
600 g veal tenderloin
1 teaspoon Szechuan
  peppercorns, crushed
1 teaspoon black
  peppercorns, crushed
1 teaspoon white
  peppercorns, crushed
salt
2 tablespoons olive oil
1/2 cup finely chopped
  fresh tarragon
1/2 cup finely chopped
  fresh thyme

CARAMELISED
WALNUT HALVES
2 tablespoons honey
1 tablespoon red wine
  vinegar
8 walnut halves

HERB OIL
1 cup finely chopped
  fresh chervil, chives
  and tarragon
1 garlic clove, mashed
2 1/2 tablespoons olive oil
2 1/2 tablespoons
  grapeseed oil

POTATO SALAD
4 golden shallots
5 tablespoons sherry
  vinegar
2 tablespoons
  brown sugar
2 1/2 tablespoons crème
  fraîche
200 g small waxy
  potatoes, boiled
  and peeled
1/4 cup chopped fresh
  chives

The day before serving, make the carpaccio. Roll the veal in all the peppercorns and salt (to taste). Place the olive oil in a very hot frying pan and sear the veal all over. Cool the veal, then roll it in the chopped tarragon and thyme. Roll the veal tightly in cling wrap and rest it overnight in the refrigerator.

To make the caramelised walnut halves, place the honey and red wine vinegar in a small saucepan over a medium heat. When it comes to the boil, add the walnuts. Remove from the heat as soon as the liquid caramelises. Dry the walnuts on a rack and keep them warm.

To make the herb oil, blend the herbs, garlic and oils in a food processor until smooth. Set aside.

Finely chop the shallots and put in a saucepan with the sherry vinegar and brown sugar. Over a high heat, reduce the liquid and leave to cool. Then mix together with the crème fraîche.

To make the potato salad, cut the potatoes into small dice, mix with the crème fraîche mixture and chives and season to taste.

Brush the leeks with a little herb oil and chargrill, then marinate in some herb oil.

Place the veal in the freezer for about a half hour before use.

To serve, place the potato salad in a circle in the centre of each plate and slice the figs around one side. Slice the carpaccio very thinly, lay it on the plate and season with rock salt. Place 2 marinated leeks on top of the potato and garnish around the plate with the seared grapes, caramelised walnuts, herb oil and aged balsamic vinegar. Finally, toss the mesclun with some herb oil, salt and pepper, arrange on top of the leek and serve.

wine suggestion
Scotchmans Hill Pinot Noir
1997.

beer suggestion
Cascade Premium.

hobayaki – grilled beef on a hoba leaf

serves 4   *Allan Koh* KOKO AT CROWN MELBOURNE

MISO is used to flavour this delicious JAPANESE GRILL.

You can use large spinach leaves instead of HOBA LEAVES

if they are not available.

main

miso

Miso, one of the most
important flavourings
in Japanese cooking, is used
in sauces, soups, marinades,
main dishes and as a table
condiment. It is basically
a rich fermented soy bean
paste and comes in a variety
of distinctive flavours and
colours. Aka miso, also
known as hatcho miso,
is strongly flavoured and dark
brown. Inaka miso is a rich,
red, country-style miso.

4 fresh hoba leaves
  or large spinach leaves,
  blanched
2 tablespoons vegetable
  oil
600 g beef tenderloin,
  diced
salt and freshly ground
  black pepper
200 g fresh shiitake
  mushrooms, cut
  in quarters
2 tablespoons sake
$1/2$ teaspoon ginger,
  grated
$1/3$ cup spring onions,
  finely sliced diagonally

HOBA MISO
4 tablespoons sake
3 tablespoons mirin
  (Japanese rice liquor)
200 g aka miso
2 tablespoons sugar
40 g inaka miso

To make the hoba miso, bring the sake and mirin to the boil
to cook the alcohol out. Combine all the hoba miso ingredients
and mix well together.

Soak the hoba leaves in water to prevent them from burning
during the cooking.

Heat the oil in a frying pan and sauté the diced beef until
medium rare. Season with salt and pepper, add the shiitake
mushrooms and deglaze with sake. Add 5 tablespoons of the
hoba miso and mix with the pan ingredients.

Transfer the sautéed beef onto the hoba or spinach leaves,
place under a preheated hot grill and cook quickly until
'medium'. Garnish the beef with the ginger and spring onions.

fresh figs poached in a citrus syrup with mascarpone ice parfait

serves 6   *Hermann Schneider* ARTHURS RESTAURANT ARTHUR'S SEAT

A perfect dish for EARLY AUTUMN when figs are at their finest.

wine suggestion
Essency Late Picked Riesling or a pinot noir champagne.

12 nice ripe black figs, peeled if preferred
4 sprigs fresh mint
1 punnet raspberries (optional)

MASCARPONE ICE PARFAIT
3 egg whites
$1/2$ cup sugar
1 tablespoon lemon juice
$3/4$ cup cream, lightly whipped
$2/3$ cup mascarpone

CITRUS SYRUP
1 cup fresh orange juice
1 cup grapefruit juice
1 cup lemon juice
2 cups sugar

To make the mascarpone ice parfait, heat the egg whites, sugar and lemon juice over a double boiler while constantly whisking vigorously, until thoroughly warmed and sugar is dissolved, to about 60°C. Then place the mixture in an electric mixer bowl and beat until cool and fluffy. Leave the meringue while you gently blend the whipped cream and mascarpone together. Fold this mixture, spoon by spoon, into the meringue mixture. Place the parfait mixture into individual moulds of your choice and freeze for about 2–4 hours before serving.

Preheat the oven to 180°C.

To make the citrus syrup, put all the juices in a non-metallic saucepan and add the sugar. Gently bring it to the boil over a low heat then add the figs. Pour syrup and figs into a baking dish and bake in the preheated oven for about 5 minutes. Remove and chill when cooled.

To serve, unmould an ice parfait on the centre of each plate. Cut each fig in half and distribute around the plates. Spoon the syrup around and garnish with mint leaves and fresh raspberries.

dessert

rhubarb and grenadine charlotte on a toffee apple galette and Williamine sorbet

serves 4   *Thomas Milligan* JJ'S BAR & GRILL AT CROWN MELBOURNE

This tasty dessert SUMS UP AUTUMN for me – the opportunity to prepare wonderful fruit such as RHUBARB and GRANNY SMITH APPLES, which are at their peak at this time of the year.

24 sponge fingers
  (4 cm x 1 cm)
icing sugar for dusting
  (optional)

CHARLOTTE
10 g unsalted butter
$^1/_3$ cup caster sugar
250 g rhubarb, leaves
  removed, diced
seeds 1 pomegranate
seeds 1 vanilla bean
5 tablespoons riesling
5 tablespoons grenadine
3 leaves gelatine
$^2/_3$ cup caster sugar
1$^1/_2$ tablespoons water
3 egg whites
1 cup whipped cream
  (soft peaks)
2 teaspoons almond oil

TOFFEE APPLE GALETTE
2 Granny Smith apples
$^2/_3$ cup icing sugar

WILLIAMINE SORBET
1$^1/_4$ cups spring water
$^1/_3$ cup caster sugar
juice 1 lemon
1 teaspoon English
  Breakfast tea leaves
1 teaspoon Calvados
1 egg white, beaten
  to soft peaks

To prepare the charlottes, heat the butter in a heavy-based saucepan and then stir in the caster sugar and cook until it has caramelised slightly. Add the rhubarb, pomegranate and vanilla seeds to the saucepan and cook until the rhubarb softens. Then add the riesling and the grenadine and reduce the mixture to syrup. Remove the saucepan from the heat and leave to cool.

Soften the gelatine leaves in a little cold water.

In a clean saucepan, boil the sugar and water until the sugar has dissolved.

Whip the egg whites to soft peaks in a very clean bowl, then continue whisking them in a steady stream as you fold through the hot sugar syrup. Add the gelatine and beat until cool.

Combine the whipped cream with the rhubarb mixture and fold in the egg white mixture. Lightly oil 4 dariel moulds (5 cm x 4 cm) with the almond oil then fill each mould with the mixture. Tap each mould on the counter to level the surface then refrigerate.

To prepare the toffee apple galettes, first preheat the oven to 160°C. Slice the cross section of the whole apples very thinly and lay the slices on silicone paper and sprinkle with the icing sugar. Bake until they caramelise and become crisp, about 20 minutes. Remove the slices from the oven and leave to cool. Store in an airtight container or they will go limp.

To prepare the sorbet, boil the water over a medium heat. Add the sugar, lemon juice and tea leaves, then remove the saucepan from the heat and leave to cool. When cold, strain off the tea leaves then add the Calvados. Gently fold in the egg white then churn the mixture in a sorbet machine according to the manufacturer's instructions. If you don't have a sorbet machine, pour the mixture into a stainless steel bowl and place it in the freezer, stirring it every hour until the mixture has frozen. Then place the sorbet in an airtight container in the freezer.

To assemble and serve, remove the charlottes from their moulds. Split the sponge fingers lengthways and carefully wrap around the charlotte. Place an apple galette onto each plate then sit a charlotte on top. With a small ice cream scoop, place a small ball of sorbet on top of each charlotte. Then place another galette at an angle to the sorbet, dust with icing sugar (if liked) and serve.

dessert

Australia is a land of great contrasts. From the tropical
north to the temperate south, the geography, climate
and local expertise all combine to produce the widest
range of meat, seafood, wine, dairy produce, fruit and
vegetables imaginable. This great storehouse gives the
imaginative chef a broad range of ingredients and colours
with which to create original culinary masterpieces.
—*Scott Webster*

In Australia we don't have regional cuisines as in other
countries – our region is the whole world. It is our
products that come from different areas, just as the
squabs in my recipe come from Glenloth Farm in Victoria.
—*Janni Kyritsis*

I work very closely with Australian suppliers of Victorian
lamb and beef and try to introduce quality Australian
produce to our guests in Dubai. I believe that the
widespread enthusiasm about Australian food produce
and cuisine that is shown by suppliers, growers and chefs
has now reached us here in the Middle East. Being able to
source quality food helps me to keep ahead in the stiffly
competitive hospitality industry.
—*Andrew Cuthbert*

Growing up in Australia has spoiled me – the variety
and quality of food that is available is exceptional – our
Victorian-grown lettuces, Barossa red wines, White Rock
veal – I could speak for ever about our produce. Call me
biased or even patriotic but I believe Australia is one
of the truly great food nations of the world.
—*David Smith*

The root of food regionalism lies in the soil and the seas
of an area, in its natural products, its seasons and nature's
gifts. And, in Tasmania, nature has been generous. While
we are famous for our exports of seafood, farmhouse
cheeses and primary products, more important to the
concept of regional food is the fact that you can still dive
along the coastal reefs and offshore islands and get a
feed of crayfish or abalone. You can still pull mussels and
oysters from the rocks, catch flounder by the light
of a torch, jag squid and net schooled anchovies and
whitebait. Quail and deer run wild, fishing boats bring
in blue fin tuna and giant west coast crabs, and fruit still
comes from the orchards that have supplied IXL jams to
the nation for over 150 years.
—*Graeme Phillips*

a winter menu

polenta with smoked

kangaroo and parmesan

◊

Kangaroo Island chicken with

hay cooked in a salt crust

◊

caramelised pineapple and

banana tart with passionfruit

sauce and coconut sorbet

wine suggestions

1996 St Hallett Blackwell Shiraz

◊

T'Gallant Unwooded

Chardonnay

◊

Angove's Late Picked

Sauvignon Blanc 'Floreate'

Pages 96–97: Cradle Mountain National Park, Tasmania.

fresh rock lobster tossed
with angel hair pasta in a light truffle sauce

serves 2   *Andrew Phillips* SHANGRI-LA HOTEL MALAYSIA

A very special starter INSPIRED by a very fresh lobster
and the availability of FRESH TRUFFLES.

court bouillon

This is a broth cooked
for 30 minutes: use 6 cups
of water, 1 cup chopped
onion, celery and carrot,
bouquet garni,
1 tablespoon lemon juice
and 2 cloves.

6 cups court bouillon
1 x 650–750 g live
   rock lobster
40 g tomatoes, peeled,
   deseeded and diced
200 g fresh angel hair
   pasta
juice $1/2$ lemon, to taste
fresh basil leaves,
   cut into thin strips
10 drops black truffle oil
1 fresh black truffle
chives, cut into
   1 cm batons

SAUCE
knob butter plus
   a little extra
2 golden shallots,
   peeled, finely chopped
$1/2$ garlic clove, minced
1 sprig fresh thyme
1 sprig fresh flat-leaf
   parsley
$1/2$ bay leaf
$1 1/2$ tablespoons
   white wine
$1 1/2$ tablespoons
   Noilly Prat
3 tablespoons fish stock
3 tablespoons cream
140 g cold butter, diced
salt and freshly ground
   black pepper
pinch cayenne pepper

To cook the lobster, put the court bouillon into a large saucepan and bring to a simmer. Plunge the lobster in, cover and cook for 6 minutes. Remove and immediately place in a bowl of iced water. Remove the claws and return them to the poaching liquid for a further 4 minutes or until cooked then refresh in the iced water. Remove the lobster tail and release the meat from the shell. It should only be about two-thirds cooked. Then release the claws and keep for a garnish. Keep the shells for future use.

To make the sauce, heat a little butter in a frying pan and gently sweat the shallots for 1 minute without colouring. Add the garlic, thyme, parsley and bay leaf and cook for a further minute without colouring. Add the white wine and reduce by a third, then add the Noilly Prat and reduce by a third. Add the fish stock and reduce by half. Add the cream and reduce by half. Whisk in the cold butter and adjust the seasoning. Strain, and if too thick, adjust with a little more fish stock then add the cayenne pepper. Set the sauce aside and keep warm.

To assemble, dice the lobster meat keeping the claws whole. Season, then heat some butter in a frying pan over a medium heat and sauté the lobster with the diced tomatoes. Cook the pasta in a large pot of rapidly boiling water for 1 minute, strain and add to the lobster in the pan. Pour in enough prepared sauce to moisten the dish then add a few drops of fresh lemon juice.

To serve, add basil and truffle oil to taste. Correct the seasoning and arrange the lobster and pasta in a serving dish or on 2 serving plates. Liberally slice the truffle over the dish, sprinkle with chives and use the shell for garnish if desired.

seared barramundi
with tomato broth and tapenade

serves 4   *Michael Hoyle* BREEZES AT CROWN MELBOURNE

A CONTEMPORARY dish, simply made. Quality ingredients create an ELEGANT meal with FINE FLAVOURS.

wine suggestion
A Clare Valley riesling
or a Hunter Valley semillon.

barramundi

If possible, it is worth the extra effort to source Robarra Springwater barramundi – it is an excellent example of a fine Australian product.

4 barramundi fillets
salt and freshly ground
  black pepper
2 teaspoons olive oil
  plus extra
1/4 cup carrot, julienned
1/4 cup celery, julienned
1/4 cup leek, julienned
1/4 cup fennel, julienned
2 tablespoons butter
4 egg-shaped (Roma)
  tomatoes, peeled,
  seeded and diced
8 black peppercorns
2 cups chicken stock
1 cup white wine
1/2 bunch chervil
  or coriander, plus extra
1/4 teaspoon saffron threads

TAPENADE
60 g kalamata olives,
  pitted
2 anchovy fillets
1 tablespoon salted
  capers
1 garlic clove
juice 1 lemon
2 1/2 tablespoons
  olive oil
freshly ground
  black pepper
4 sprigs basil

Preheat the oven to 180°C.

To make the tapenade, blend all the ingredients together in a food processor.

To cook the barramundi, season the fillets and brush with the olive oil. In a frying pan, sauté the vegetables in the butter over a medium heat. Combine the tomatoes, peppercorns, stock, wine and chervil (stems only) or coriander in a saucepan. Simmer for 15 minutes, strain and then add the vegetables and saffron. Leave to infuse for 10 minutes. Coat a non-stick frying pan with a light film of olive oil, heat over a high heat then add the fish fillets and sear until browned and crisp, about 4 minutes. Finish cooking in the oven for 3 minutes.

To serve, mound the vegetables equally between 4 wide-rimmed bowls. Add a small amount of broth. Place a barramundi fillet on top of each vegetable mound. Spoon some tapenade on top of each barramundi fillet. Garnish with fresh sprigs of the chervil or coriander.

salad of roast duck, watercress, pecans and burnt orange vinaigrette

serves 4

Philip Johnson E'CCO BISTRO BRISBANE

Warm salad is one of my FAVOURITE DISHES. Combining a HOT meat component with COLD salad ingredients makes it a GREAT LUNCH dish. LIGHT, yet filling, and you are still able to make it back to work.

wine suggestion
1995 St Huberts Roussane, Yarra Valley, Victoria.

beer suggestion
Crown Lager.

1 x 1.6 kg free-range duck, Bendele if possible
1 bay leaf
$^1/_2$ cinnamon stick
6 cloves garlic, unpeeled and lightly crushed
4 sprigs fresh thyme
$^1/_2$ lemon
sea salt flakes and freshly ground black pepper

BURNT ORANGE VINAIGRETTE
$2^1/_2$ cups orange juice, freshly squeezed
$2^1/_2$ tablespoons extra virgin olive oil
sea salt flakes and freshly ground black pepper

SALAD
4 seedless navel oranges
1 witlof (Belgian endive), leaves separated
2 handfuls rocket, stems removed
1 large handful watercress
$^1/_2$ red onion, peeled and finely sliced
$^3/_4$ cup pecans, roasted

Preheat the oven to 200°C.

To roast the duck, remove and discard the duck neck, rinse and dry the duck inside and out. Place the bay leaf, cinnamon, garlic and thyme inside the duck. Rub the duck skin well with lemon and season with salt and pepper. Place the duck in a roasting dish and roast for 20 minutes, basting occasionally with the pan juices.

In the meantime, make the burnt orange vinaigrette. Boil the orange juice in a heavy-based saucepan until reduced to $^3/_4$ cup, then remove it from the heat and cool slightly before whisking in the olive oil. Season to taste with salt and pepper.

Reduce the oven temperature to 150°C and roast the duck for a further 50 minutes. Continue to baste.

To make the salad, peel the oranges, removing all the pith, and finely slice them into a total of 16 x 6 mm thick rounds. Wash, pick and spin-dry the witlof, rocket and watercress. Combine the salad leaves, onions and pecans in a large bowl with just enough vinaigrette to moisten.

Remove the duck from the oven and allow to rest in a warm place for 10 minutes before carving. Remove the legs and breast from the duck, and halve the breast diagonally. If the duck is cooked in advance, reheat it under a hot grill.

To serve, trim the meat from the legs into several pieces and discard the bones. Halve each section of breast meat. Arrange three slices of orange on each plate and top with leg meat. Share the salad between the plates, and sit it on top of the duck. Top the salad with a final orange slice and the duck breast. Drizzle a little extra orange vinaigrette over and around the plate.

polenta with smoked kangaroo and parmesan

serves 4 ·   *Maggie Beer* MAGGIE BEER FARM SHOP NURIOOTPA

I first started SMOKING KANGAROO when it became legal in South Australia at least 15 years ago. To me it was the natural extension of MARRYING a BAROSSA, that is, a Silesian tradition of preserving and smoking food with REGIONAL INGREDIENTS.

wine suggestion
St Hallett Blackwell Shiraz 1996.

1 x 150 g piece parmesan cheese
3 cups chicken stock
185 g polenta
1½ teaspoons salt
butter
4 tablespoons extra virgin olive oil
200 g very thinly sliced smoked kangaroo, if available (or prosciutto)
2 handfuls rocket
good quality balsamic vinegar (optional)

Preheat the oven to 150°C.

To cook the polenta, grate 100 g of the parmesan and set it aside. Heat the stock in a deep saucepan until simmering then pour in the polenta and salt, stirring constantly. Stir the polenta over a very gentle heat for about 20 minutes, until it begins to leave the sides of the pan, then add the grated parmesan. Tip the polenta into an ovenproof bowl, then dot with a little butter and put it in the oven, covered, to keep warm.

Warm the olive oil gently in a frying pan and quickly toss the kangaroo slices in it. The pan should not be too hot or the kangaroo will discolour and spoil.

To serve, turn the warm polenta out onto a serving platter and mound the kangaroo and rocket around it. Shave the remaining parmesan over the lot with a potato peeler. Add a drizzle of balsamic vinegar, if liked.

roast Glenloth game squab
with heart and liver cabbage rolls

serves 6   *Janni Kyritsis* MG GARAGE RESTAURANT SYDNEY

With the INCREASING CHILL in the air my thoughts turn towards game. This dish is a favourite way of SERVING SQUAB, with HEARTY cabbage rolls.

6 squabs
salt and freshly ground
   black pepper
olive oil

SQUAB STOCK
trimmings from squabs
1/2 cup chopped onion
1/2 cup chopped carrot
1/4 cup chopped celery
2 cloves garlic
2 cups water

CABBAGE ROLLS
hearts and livers from
   the squabs
2 tablespoons butter
1 tablespoon brandy
1 small onion, chopped
100 g bacon, diced
1 clove garlic, chopped
150 g cabbage, diced
6 tablespoons
   breadcrumbs, toasted in
   1 tablespoon butter
2 tablespoons fresh
   parsley, chopped
1/2 teaspoon fresh thyme
   leaves
salt and freshly ground
   black pepper
6 large cabbage leaves,
   cut in half

SAUCE
1/4 cup brandy
1 cup red wine
about 2 cups squab
   stock, hot
4 slices orange peel, pith
   removed
salt and freshly ground
   black pepper
pinch crushed juniper
   berries
2 tablespoons butter

Preheat the oven to 200°C.

Remove the insides of the squabs and reserve the heart and liver for the stuffing. Cut off the neck, wings and feet. Rinse and pat dry the squab and trimmings.

To make the squab stock, roast the squab trimmings with the vegetables in a greased baking pan in the preheated oven until brown. Place baking pan on the cooktop, deglaze the pan with the water and transfer the mixture to a small saucepan. Cover and simmer for about 1 hour. Strain the stock through a fine sieve and reserve.

To make the cabbage rolls, sauté the heart and liver quickly in half the butter and deglaze the pan with the brandy. Remove from the pan. In the same pan, sauté the onion and bacon in the remaining butter until soft. Add the garlic and diced cabbage and cook further, until the cabbage is cooked. Mix all the ingredients together except the cabbage leaves, and season with salt and pepper. Blanch the cabbage leaves in boiling water for 1 minute and refresh. Discard the tough parts. Lay the cabbage leaves out flat, place a spoonful of stuffing on each leaf and make the cabbage rolls. Cover and set aside. Steam them in a steamer for 20 minutes before serving.

Preheat the oven to 250°C. To roast the squabs, season the squabs inside and out with salt and pepper and rub with olive oil. Place in an oiled oven pan and cook until golden brown, about 15 minutes. Keep in a warm place to rest for 10 minutes. The breasts should remain pink.

To make the sauce, discard the fat from the oven pan, then place the pan on the cooktop and deglaze with the brandy and the red wine. Bring to the boil and add the hot stock and orange peel. Reduce the sauce to 1 1/2 cups fast, over a high heat. Season with salt, pepper and crushed juniper berries. Finish the sauce by whisking in the butter.

To serve, carve the breast and legs from each squab and place on top of the cabbage rolls on warm serving plates. Pour the sauce over and serve immediately.

wine suggestion
1998 Spring Vale Pinot Noir, Tasmania.

main

twice cooked duck with
buckwheat noodles, orange and ginger jam

serves 2   *David Smith* TREETOPS RESTAURANT MALOLO ISLAND FIJI

I am REALLY FANATICAL about duck and always buy the finest quality available. I like to buy mine from the Game Farm, New South Wales. This dish is great to serve for a SPECIAL MEAL as the duck and jam can be made in advance.

wine suggestion
A full-bodied wine such as a Peter Lehman shiraz.

beer suggestion
Fiji Bitter or Cascade Premium Lager.

1 x size 18 duck
2 medium hot chillies, seeded and chopped
salt
1 tablespoon peanut oil
200 g buckwheat noodles, cooked and kept warm
1 bunch Chinese broccoli or spinach leaves, steamed just before serving

ORANGE AND GINGER JAM
3 navel oranges, peeled, pith removed, roughly chopped
1 small knob fresh ginger, peeled and chopped
1 cup orange juice
1 1/2 tablespoons sugar
1 clove

DUCK STOCK
1 celery stick, diced
1 medium carrot, diced
2 white onions, diced
1 cup strong chicken stock

Preheat the oven to 200°C.

To cook the duck, season it all over with the chillies and salt. Roast on an oven tray in the preheated oven for 10 minutes then reduce the oven temperature to 160°C and cook for a further 30 minutes. Set aside to cool.

Debone the duck carefully, retaining the supreme (half wing) bone. Reserve the bones for the stock.

To make the jam, combine all the jam ingredients in a saucepan and simmer for 20–25 minutes, or until the mixture is thick and syrupy. Remove from the heat and set aside.

To make the duck stock, combine the reserved duck bones and stock ingredients in a saucepan and bring to the boil over a high heat. Reduce the temperature and simmer for 1 hour. Remove from the heat and strain through a fine sieve.

Sauté the duck pieces in the peanut oil in a frying pan over a high heat, then deglaze with the duck stock.

To serve, place the noodles in the centre of each plate, top with a little steamed Chinese broccoli or spinach leaves and place a duck breast and leg in the centre. Dot the jam around the plate and drizzle over the reduced duck glaze.

rare loin of venison with
warm potato salad and braised red cabbage

serves 4   *Liam Tomlin* BANC SYDNEY

Braised red cabbage MATCHES GAME BEAUTIFULLY.

I recommend serving the VENISON RARE.

500 g kipfler potatoes

480 g loin of venison,
   from thinner end of loin

salt and freshly ground
   black pepper

5 teaspoons vegetable oil

50 g lardons of bacon

3 golden shallots, sliced

1 tablespoon grain
   mustard

1 small bunch fresh
   rocket leaves

5 tablespoons red wine jus

10 g sliced fresh chives

BRAISED RED CABBAGE

100 g butter

1/2 red cabbage, thinly
   sliced

2 1/2 tablespoons Forum
   Cabernet Sauvignon red
   wine vinegar, if
   available, plus 2 1/2
   tablespoons red wine
   vinegar

juice 1 orange

2/3 cup port

1/2 stick cinnamon

4 teaspoons demerara
   sugar

salt and freshly ground
   black pepper

BALSAMIC DRESSING

1 egg yolk

2 teaspoons Dijon mustard

1 1/2 tablespoons balsamic
   vinegar

2/3 cup vegetable oil

2/3 cup olive oil

salt and freshly ground
   black pepper

1/2 lemon

Preheat the oven to 170°C.

To prepare the red cabbage, melt the butter in a heavy-based saucepan then add the red cabbage and cook until the cabbage wilts down without colouring. Add the 2 vinegars, orange juice, port, cinnamon and sugar, then season with salt and pepper. Continue to cook over a medium heat until all liquid has evaporated. Cover with a silicone paper lid and transfer to the preheated oven. Cook for a further 45 minutes. Remove from the oven and keep warm, then turn the oven up to 220°C.

Prepare the potatoes while the cabbage is cooking. Wash the potatoes and cook them in salted water until tender, about 15–20 minutes. Drain and cool slightly then peel and slice into 1 cm slices.

To make the balsamic dressing, mix the egg yolk, mustard and vinegar in a bowl and whisk together. Add both the oils to form an emulsion and season to taste with salt and pepper and lemon juice.

To cook the venison, season it with salt and pepper. Heat 2 teaspoons of vegetable oil in a baking pan and seal the venison until golden brown all over. Transfer to the oven and continue to cook for a further 4–5 minutes or longer if you prefer your meat cooked more. Remove the venison from the oven and allow to rest for 10 minutes in a warm place before carving.

To make the potato salad, heat the remaining vegetable oil in a frying pan and add the lardons of bacon and cook until golden brown. Add the shallots and potatoes and cook until they take on a light golden colour. Add the mustard and balsamic dressing and toss gently. Add the rocket and toss the salad so that it just wilts. Remove from the heat and season to taste. Place the salad in a sieve to allow any excess oil to drain off.

To serve, warm the red wine jus and carve the venison into 16 even slices. Lightly season them with salt and pepper. Place a 6 cm pastry cutter in the centre of each plate and spoon the potato salad into it, pressing down on it so it will hold together once the cutter is removed. Lay 4 slices of venison on top of each salad, overlapping to form a nice circle of meat, then remove the pastry cutter. Make a quenelle of cabbage between two tablespoons and place on top of the venison. Pour the red wine jus over and around the venison. Garnish with the sliced chives.

wine suggestion

My wine suggestion for this dish is a 1996 Dromana Estate Reserve Pinot Noir from the Mornington Peninsula, Victoria.

seared breast of wood pigeon, ravioli of porcini and pigeon, game and hazelnut jus

serves 12   *James Brotherston & Antony Scholtmeyer* JAMESON'S RESTAURANT BRISBANE

This is a dish about FLAVOUR and TEXTURE. We use the whole bird – the BREASTS SIT LIKE A CROWN on the ravioli.

wine suggestion

I prefer to drink grenache with this dish. Hardy's Tintara Grenache 1996 or 1997 would be my first choice, yet I also like a very full pinot. The pinot would most likely be Dry River, Pegasus Bay, or Felton Road from New Zealand, or Calera from California. If Australian, 1994 Bannockburn Serré Pinot Noir, 1994 Giaconda or Yarra Ridge Reserve Pinot Noir.

tip

The ravioli is stuffed with the meat from the rest of the bird and porcini mushrooms. We make the sauce from the bones – it is a game-reduced stock that we drizzle hazelnut purée into. This jus links the meat and the porcini mushroom flavours.

12 whole pigeons
1 onion, roughly chopped
1 carrot, roughly chopped
1 celery stalk, roughly chopped
4 cloves garlic, crushed
1 juniper berry
8 sprigs fresh thyme
4 fresh bay leaves
salt and freshly ground black pepper
4 cups water
2 tablespoons olive oil, plus extra for cooking
1 1/2 cups red wine
3 golden shallots, diced
100 g can porcini mushrooms, drained
1 packet gow gee wrappers
egg wash (1 egg yolk, beaten)

BRAISED RED CABBAGE
1 onion, halved and finely sliced
1/2 red cabbage, shredded
100 ml red wine vinegar
3 tablespoons cumberland sauce

HAZELNUT COULIS
3/4 cup ground hazelnuts
100 ml verjuice
2 1/2 tablespoons hazelnut oil

Preheat the oven to 250°C.

To make the pigeon stock, debone the pigeon breasts and legs and set aside. Remove the skin from the breasts. Reserve. Roast the carcasses in the oven for 20 minutes, then add half the onion, carrot, celery, garlic, juniper berry, herbs and season with salt and pepper. Cook until golden brown, cover with water and braise for 4 hours, adding more water if necessary. Strain and reserve stock. Reduce the oven temperature to 150°C.

To cook the pigeon legs and make the braised stock, seal the legs in an oiled frying pan. Add the remaining vegetables and brown. Deglaze the pan with red wine and add the pigeon stock. Reduce the liquid by three-quarters. Place the pigeon legs and braised stock in a casserole and cook in the oven for about 3 1/2 hours, or until tender. Remove the legs from the stock, cool, and debone, reserving the meat and braised stock.

Sweat shallots and porcini mushrooms in an oiled frying pan over a medium heat, add half the braising stock and reduce until it thickens. Add pigeon meat and remove from the heat. Season and cool. Reduce remainder of the stock and reserve for the sauce.

To make the ravioli, place a gow gee wrapper on a lightly floured bench and dollop a spoon of meat in the middle. Brush the gow gee edges with a little egg wash, top with another wrapper and press the edges together firmly. Repeat until you have made all the ravioli. Just before serving, poach the ravioli, 3 at a time, in plenty of simmering water for 2 minutes.

To make the braised red cabbage, sweat the onion in an oiled frying pan until it is transparent. Add the cabbage, and when just wilted, deglaze pan with red wine vinegar. Reduce the vinegar to a syrup, add the cumberland sauce and cook until it thickens and sticks to the cabbage. Season and keep warm.

To make the hazelnut coulis, blend the hazelnuts and verjuice until it is a smooth purée. Add extra verjuice if necessary. Slowly blend in the hazelnut oil. Season with salt and pepper. The consistency should be like thick, pourable cream.

To serve. Seal the pigeon breast in a hot oiled frying pan for 1 minute on each side. Place a small amount of red cabbage on each plate. Drizzle a little hazelnut coulis around the cabbage. Put 1 (or more) ravioli beside the cabbage. Slice the pigeon breast across and lay 4 slices on top of the ravioli. Drizzle the reduced braised stock around the plates.

Australian beef fillet tagine style with pumpkin and lentil ragout and honeyed beef jus

serves 4   *Andrew Cuthbert* DUBAI HILTON

I like to EXPERIMENT with local produce and cooking styles. This dish uses AUSTRALIAN BEEF and is based on TRADITIONAL MOROCCAN tagine dishes.

main

tip
Middle Eastern cooking techniques vary quite dramatically, from cooking whole camels in giant sand ovens to baking fish wrapped in dates over charcoal fires. In our region we include Indian spices and techniques in the local cooking, giving an even greater diversity of flavours.

4 x 170 g Australian beef
   fillets, trimmed
fresh coriander leaves
rock salt
1/2 cup blanched whole
   almonds, dry roasted

POACHING LIQUID
2 cups chicken stock
10 threads saffron
1 onion, quartered
10 white peppercorns
1 carrot, chopped
2 bay leaves

PUMPKIN RAGOUT
2 garlic cloves, minced
1 onion, finely chopped
1 tablespoon olive oil
1 cup sprouted green
   lentils or plain green
   lentils, cooked
4 cups pumpkin, cooked
   and diced
2 tomatoes, peeled, diced
   and blanched
1/2 teaspoon ground
   cinnamon
salt and freshly ground
   black pepper

SAUCE
2 cups beef jus
1/2 cup sultanas, soaked
1 tablespoon honey
1 tablespoon butter

To make the poaching liquid, put all the ingredients into a large saucepan and bring to a simmer. Poach the beef fillet in this liquid for 8–10 minutes for medium (or to desired) doneness.

To make the ragout, sauté the garlic and onions in the olive oil then toss in the lentils, pumpkin and tomatoes and cook together until heated through. Add a little cinnamon and seasoning to taste.

To make the sauce, put the beef jus in a saucepan and bring it to a simmer. Add the sultanas and honey, then at the last minute whisk in the butter to finish the sauce.

To serve, on each serving plate place the pumpkin ragout in the centre then top with the poached beef. Sauce the plate, then garnish with the coriander and top the beef with the rock salt. Scatter the almonds around the sauce.

Kangaroo Island chicken
with hay cooked in a salt crust

serves 4   *Robert Castellani* DONOVANS MELBOURNE

This chicken dish is SPECTACULAR to serve with its

SALT CRUST AND HAY EXTERIOR. The salt crust is torn apart

at the table to expose the PERFECTLY COOKED CHOOK.

main

wine suggestion

A soft chardonnay, probably T'Gallant Unwooded Chardonnay from the Mornington Peninsula in Victoria; serve almost at room temperature.

Kangaroo Island chicken

Kangaroo Island chicken is the most magnificent chicken to cook with and to eat – a true free-range bird. You can really taste the difference that good farming makes.

1 free-range chicken, Kangaroo Island or the best you can afford
olive oil
freshly ground black pepper
300 g field mushrooms, cleaned and roughly sliced
250 g fresh grapes, stalks removed and squashed
hay or dried herbs
sprigs fresh rosemary from 1 bunch
sprigs fresh oregano from 1 bunch
egg wash (1 egg yolk beaten with scant water)

SALT CRUST
8 cups plain flour
6 egg whites
2 cups salt
water

Preheat the oven to 180°C.

To make the crust, combine the flour, egg whites and salt in a food processor or blender. Blend until it resembles breadcrumbs. Add enough water to form into a dough. Remove the dough and knead for 5 minutes, then shape into a ball.

To cook the chicken, wash and dry the inside and outside of the chicken. Brush the chicken all over with the olive oil and season with pepper. Place the mushrooms and grapes inside the chicken cavity.

Roll out the dough in an oblong shape to about 8 mm thick on a lightly floured surface. Make a bed of some of the hay and fresh herbs on one side of the soft dough and set the chicken on top of it. Form the dough around the bottom of the chicken. Place some hay and fresh herbs around and over the chicken. Then roll the dough over the top and wrap it around the chicken completely. Brush the edges of the dough either side of where the dough meets with egg wash and press down with your fingers to seal well.

Place the dough-wrapped chicken seam-side down on an oiled baking tray and bake for 1½ hours. Remove the tray from the oven and leave the chicken to rest for 15 minutes.

To serve, place the chicken on a serving dish and present triumphantly to your guests. Cut around the circumference of the salt crust and lift off the top with the hay. The guests will enjoy the steaming aroma. Take the chicken back to the kitchen, lift it out of the salt crust and discard all the hay and herbs. Cut the chicken into 4 portions and serve on warm plates, accompanied by the mushrooms and grapes from the filling and the tender juices flowing from the cut chicken.

Serve with peeled waxy potatoes that have been rolled in hot walnut oil and butter, and butter beans rolled in parsley and olive oil.

black rice and palm sugar pudding

serves 6   *Cheong Liew* THE GRANGE RESTAURANT ADELAIDE HILTON
CONSULTANT CHEF PARMELIA HILTON PERTH

This dish was created by MY WIFE MARY when she discovered the SRI LANKAN PALM SUGAR custard. It is a tribute to her that so many have adapted it for their own menus. The NUTTY flavour and texture of the rice BLENDS beautifully with the soft custard.

wine suggestion

1998 Rymill June Traminer from Coonawarra, South Australia.

6 pears
4 cups sugar syrup
(dissolve equal
quantities of sugar and
water over a medium
heat and cool)
1 vanilla bean
icing sugar for dusting

BLACK RICE
1/3 cup black rice
200 ml water
pinch salt

CARAMEL
1/3 cup caster sugar
5 tablespoons water

CUSTARD
2 cups milk
1 cup desiccated coconut
1/3 cup palm sugar
2 eggs
4 egg yolks

To cook the black rice, add the black rice to the water in a heavy-based saucepan, then add the salt. Bring to the boil, reduce to a simmer and cook until tender, that is, the rice splits open, about 1–2 hours. Some varieties of black rice take a long time to cook, so be prepared and remember to top up with more water when necessary.

To make the caramel, mix the sugar and water together over a medium heat, stirring occasionally, until the mixture turns a dark caramel colour. Remove from the heat as soon as it turns brown. It will keep cooking away from the heat. Do not stir, but brush the sides of the saucepan with cold water to incorporate all the sugar. If you would like it a little browner, put it back over the heat.

Clean and lightly oil 6 x 100 ml moulds and line them with the caramel. Allow to cool. The remaining caramel becomes the pouring sauce – to prevent it from setting, dilute with water until the caramel has the consistency of sauce.

To make the custard, first preheat the oven to 150°C. Scald the milk and add the desiccated coconut and palm sugar. Let this mixture stand for 30 minutes, then strain. Lightly beat together the eggs and egg yolks. Pour the warm milk into the eggs. Pour half this mixture into the moulds and cook in a bain-marie or place the moulds in 2 cm of simmering water in a baking pan in the oven. Just before the mixture is completely set, about 30 minutes, add a layer of black rice and then another layer of the custard mixture. Now cook until set – about 40 minutes. Chill in the refrigerator.

To poach the pears, heat the sugar syrup with the vanilla bean to simmering, then add the pears. When cooked, slice each pear into 4 pieces lengthways, retaining the pear shape. Dust with icing sugar and place in a hot oven until caramelised.

To serve, unmould the puddings by submerging each mould in warm water. Carefully turn the moulds out onto serving plates. Pour over a little diluted caramel sauce and serve each with a roasted pear.

dessert

caramelised pineapple and banana tart with passionfruit sauce and coconut sorbet

serves 10–12　　　　*Marieke Brugman* HOWQUA DALE GOURMET RETREAT

This tart is DELICIOUS hot or cold. I use Bethonga Gold PINEAPPLES from Queensland which are ALWAYS RELIABLE and GOLDEN SWEET.

CARAMELISED PINEAPPLE
1 large pineapple, peeled, cored, and cut into 8 slices
1 cup palm sugar, grated
$1/3$ cup brown rum
juice and finely grated zest 2 limes (reserve zest for pastry)
75 g butter

BANANAS
6 bananas, peeled, sliced in half lengthways
2 tablespoons sugar
2 tablespoons Mandarin Napoleon liqueur
50 g butter, melted
juice 1 lemon
1 teaspoon pure vanilla extract

PASTRY
100 g unsalted butter
$1/4$ cup caster sugar
reserved lime zest
1 small egg
$1^1/4$ cups flour

FILLING FOR TART
125 g unsalted butter
$3/4$ cup icing sugar, sieved
2 eggs
1 teaspoon pure vanilla extract
2 tablespoons coconut liqueur
$1^1/4$ cups fresh, finely ground blanched almonds

COCONUT SORBET
2 cups sugar syrup (made by boiling an equal quantity of sugar and water until just dissolved)
2 cups coconut cream, Mae Ploy if available
juice 2 limes
2 tablespoons coconut liqueur

PASSIONFRUIT SAUCE
1 cup sugar
pulp from 8–10 juicy passionfruit

Preheat the oven to 220°C.

To caramelise the pineapple, combine the palm sugar with the rum, lime juice and butter and gently heat to dissolve. Coat the pineapple slices with this marinade, place them in a shallow baking pan lined with baking paper and cover with the remaining marinade. Bake for 1 hour in the preheated oven, turning once, until the pineapple slices are caramelised. Drain and reserve any juices.

To cook the bananas, place them in a shallow baking pan lined with baking paper. Combine the sugar, liqueur, butter, lemon juice and vanilla, pour over the bananas, cover with foil and bake for 15 minutes, turning once. Drain and reserve any juices.

To make the pastry for the tart, cream the butter and sugar with the lime zest in a food processor. Add the egg and process. Add the flour and process until the dough comes together in a ball. Remove and quickly knead into a disc, cover with cling wrap and refrigerate for at least 1 hour before rolling out on a lightly floured board into a circle to fit the top of a 28 cm ovenproof pan.

To make the tart filling, cream the butter and sugar until light and fluffy. Beat in the eggs, vanilla extract and coconut liqueur, then fold in the ground almond. Set aside.

To assemble the tart, reduce the oven temperature to 175°C. Line the base of the ovenproof pan with baking paper. Arrange the pineapple and the banana on the bottom, then cover with the filling. Place the pastry top over the filling. Rest the tart in the refrigerator for 1 hour. Bake the tart for 50–60 minutes in the preheated oven, until the pastry is golden and crisp and the filling has set. Invert the tart onto a large flat plate.

To make the coconut sorbet, combine all the ingredients and churn in an ice cream machine following the manufacturer's instructions.

To make the passionfruit sauce, cover the sugar with just enough water to moisten, dissolve over a gentle heat then bring to the boil and cook to a deep caramel. Remove from heat and carefully add the passionfruit pulp. Cook over a gentle heat, stirring continously to amalgamate. Cool.

Slice the tart into portions, drizzle a little passionfruit sauce alongside and add a scoop of coconut sorbet. The reserved fruit juices can be combined and gently reheated as a second sauce.

wine suggestion
Angove's Late Picked Sauvignon Blanc 'Floreate' combines citrus characteristics with viscosity which provides a light foil to the intensity of the pineapple.

dessert

hot chocolate banana pudding with preserved kumquats and King Island crème fraîche

serves 4   *Scott Webster* RESTAURANT MOSAIC SYDNEY

This is a RICH, DARK CHOCOLATE pudding accompanied by preserved KUMQUATS which give a jaffa-like taste. This is offset by the slight sourness of the King Island CRÈME FRAÎCHE.

wine suggestion

1998 Rosemount Estate Syrah.

2 or 4 spring roll skins
icing sugar
1 cup King Island
   crème fraîche
icing sugar (optional)

PRESERVED KUMQUATS
4 cups Australian red wine
2 cups sugar
10 cinnamon pods
10 star anise, whole
1 kg kumquats, seeded
   and sliced
2 oranges, thinly sliced
2 lemons, thinly sliced

CHOCOLATE PUDDING
100 g dark chocolate
60 g butter
1/4 cup cocoa powder
4 eggs, separated
6 teaspoons sugar
30 g bananas, mashed
knob butter
flour for dusting

To make the preserved kumquats, put the red wine, sugar, cinnamon and star anise in a saucepan over a moderate heat and bring to the boil. Pour it over the fruits in a bowl and allow to macerate, covered, for 24 hours. Chill and reserve.

To make the puddings, melt the chocolate and butter together in a double boiler or in a bowl placed in simmering water. Stir in the cocoa powder. Slowly add the yolks to the melted chocolate.

Whisk the egg whites in a clean bowl with the sugar to form stiff peaks. Into this, carefully fold the bananas and then the chocolate mixture. Butter and flour 4 x 6 cm ramekin dishes and line with the spring roll skins. Spoon the chocolate mixture evenly into the skins. Freeze until required.

Preheat the oven to 200°C.

Bake the frozen puddings in the preheated oven for 9–10 minutes. After baking, remove the puddings from the ramekin dishes.

To serve, place each hot chocolate pudding on a serving plate and dust with icing sugar. Add a scoop of crème fraîche and some of the kumquats and their sauce and dust with icing sugar if desired.

dessert

hot apricot and vanilla soft-centred pudding served on apricot and sauterne sauce with cuvée riche ice cream

serves 6   *Gary Cooper* ELEONORE'S RESTAURANT CHÂTEAU YERING YARRA VALLEY

A rich, REFRESHING dessert tasting of apricot, toasted almond and vanilla with a SPLENDID CUVÉE RICHE ice cream.

cuvée riche

This is a sparkling champagne-style wine from Domaine Chandon in the Yarra Valley. When combined with local free-range eggs and thick cream, it makes a rich and delicious ice cream.

250 g butter,
  plus a little extra
4 teaspoons flour, plus
  a little extra
240 g white chocolate
4 egg yolks
4 whole eggs
1/2 cup sugar
1/3 cup flaked almonds,
  dry roasted

APRICOT AND SAUTERNE SAUCE
3/4 cup dried apricots
2/3 cup water
5 tablespoons sauterne
2 1/2 tablespoons sugar
  syrup (dissolve equal
  parts of sugar and water
  and cool)

CUVÉE RICHE ICE CREAM
1 vanilla bean, split
  and scraped
4 cups thick cream
20 egg yolks
1 1/4 cups sugar
3 cups Domaine Chandon
  Cuvée Riche, if available,
  or sparkling wine,
  reduced to just under
  1 cup

Preheat the oven to 200°C.

To make the chocolate pudding, butter and flour the 6 moulds (1/3 cup size). Melt the 250 g butter and the white chocolate together in a double boiler or a bowl placed in a saucepan of simmering water. Remove from heat. In another bowl, whisk the egg yolks, eggs and sugar together until fluffy. Gently fold the egg mix into the chocolate butter. Sift and stir the 4 teaspoons flour through the mixture.

To make the apricot and sauterne sauce, combine the apricots and water in a saucepan, bring to the boil over a low heat and simmer until the water evaporates and the apricots are soft. Add the sauterne and sugar syrup. Purée in a food processor and strain through a fine sieve. Reserve in a warm place.

Half fill the moulds with the chocolate pudding mixture, add about 1 tablespoon of apricot and sauterne purée then fill to the top with more chocolate mix. Bake in the preheated oven for 12 minutes and set aside in a warm place.

To make the custard for the ice cream, place the vanilla bean and the cream in a saucepan and bring to the boil. Remove immediately from the heat. In a separate bowl, whisk together the egg yolks, sugar, and wine reduction until light and fluffy. Strain the cream to remove the vanilla bean, and pour it into the egg mixture, whisking all the time. Pour back into the saucepan and return to the stove over a low heat. Using a wooden spoon, continually stir the custard until it begins to thicken and coats the back of the spoon. Remove from the heat and refrigerate until cold then churn in an ice cream maker according to the manufacturer's instructions. Makes about 7 cups.

To serve, pour some apricot and sauterne sauce at room temperature in the centre of each plate. Turn the puddings out of their moulds and put the puddings to one side of the serves, with a scoop of ice cream on the other side. Garnish the pudding with the roasted almonds.

spring

spring

SPRING does not arrive suddenly in Australia. Winter SLIPS SLOWLY away, and 'we become aware that the GREAT WALL of the AUSTRALIAN SUMMER is approaching as great CASCADES of WATTLE line the roads,' wrote Maggie Alderson. Escoffier dipped WATTLE FLOWERS in batter, and DEEP FRIED them.

—Tony Bilson

He then dusted the beignets with sugar and served them with tea.

Spring arrives more dramatically in southern Australia and one of my fondest memories is of the new spring vegetables at Victoria markets. Artichokes, vibrant green asparagus and tender young broad beans together with the flowers make for an experience that excites the senses. Although Sydney now has a grower's market, Melbourne and Adelaide have special treasures with their central markets – they play an important part in the life and the quality of cooking of both cities.

Australian lamb is at its best in spring and the one meal we have that is as powerfully traditional as the Pot au Feu is The Sunday Roast. Paul Wilson has taken the classic Provençale flavours of lamb and anchovy and combined them to celebrate Saskia Beer's Barossa Valley milk-fed lamb. Gary Cooper captures the spirit with his Koonawarra kid. Peter Doyle uses the end of the winter citrus season to create a dish with the colours of a bush-fire sunset, the blood oranges anticipating summer.

—Tony Bilson

I remember as a young boy growing up in Maitland, New South Wales, my grandmother growing huge quantities of rhubarb – so much that many of the neighbours were given free rations. She cooked it in a slow oven with a touch of water and some sugar. I still recall the aroma of the freshly stewed fruit straight from the oven. The first pink stems of the season were eagerly awaited. The end of the rhubarb season, although sad, meant that summer was well on the way – time for fresh lemons and mulberries! Our garden grew all kinds of fruit and vegetables – enough for us and the neighbours. Having a garden full of food seemed a natural way of life. This exposure to great food and drink encouraged and inspired me to cook and this continues to this day.

—John Torode

I love the Yarra Valley for its gorgeous countryside, wonderful wines and great cheeses – there is no better place to be on a sunny day in Victoria. The windswept green fields of King Island remind me of Scotland, but the cheeses on this emerald isle are much better.

—Marcus Moore

Working for at least half of my 25-year career away from Australia has made me very aware of our magnificent and diverse quality food produce. For lamb, I love the Gippsland area; for cheese there is Tasmania and the great goat's cheese from Western Australia; and Queensland, Victoria and Tasmania have wonderful seafood. The wines I love are the boutique wines from the Mornington Peninsula, Yarra Valley and Western Australia.
—*Michael Mangan*

Verjuice has been around since Roman times, and was taken up by the French with such a passion that it was equivalent to the soy sauce of the Asian kitchen. As vignerons, we began making our own verjuice commercially in 1984. It seemed the perfect product for a partnership – I was a passionate cook, we had a farm restaurant and we had a vineyard. It made sense to use every bit of our produce.

Verjuice has become a real staple of my cooking. As a juice of grapes, picked green and stabilised, it's used as a mild acidulant. It doesn't mask the flavour of the food it's teamed with as stronger acidulants, such as lemon juice and vinegar, do. I make a vinaigrette with it added to extra virgin olive oil, walnut or almond oils. I brush it over grilled foods or deglaze chicken or seafood with it. I also add it to stocks and sauces or make a quivering jelly with it. It's the most versatile cooking ingredient I know!
—*Maggie Beer*

The Mornington Peninsula, with its hills, has a diversity of microclimates and has recently changed from being a mainly apple and stone fruit growing area to a predominantly vine grape and berry fruit producing area. There has also been a great resurgence of market gardens on the lower plains of Rosebud and Boneo, and they produce an abundance of many varieties of vegetables. The small-acreage farms have great appeal for retired people who are creating specialist and niche market produce such as avocadoes, sour cherries, olives, quinces, and hydroponic products (lettuces, herbs and tomatoes). Port Phillip Bay supplies us with a variety of less commercial fish such as garfish, flathead, King George whiting, calamari, mussels and (infrequently) snapper and sand crabs.
—*Hermann Schneider*

Great food is all about flavour – taking several key ingredients and combining them to allow each flavour to speak for itself. I never add that extra herb or garnish to my food as it has no 'eat' value, so why is it there?
—*Philip Johnson*

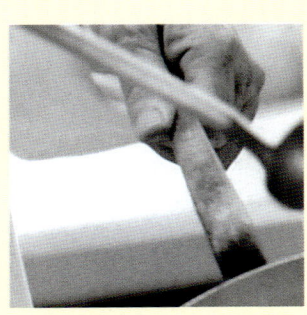

a spring menu

seared calamari with bitter

green salad, five-spiced

chilli salt, palm sugar

and lime dressing

◊

roasted new season Barossa

lamb with pissaladière tart,

broadbeans and extra virgin

olive oil sauce

◊

rhubarb crostata with pecans

wine suggestion

Leo Buring's Leonay Riesling,

Eden Valley, South Australia

◊

Brown Brothers Muscat

will complement the crostata

Pages 132–133: Field of flowers in Oberon, New South Wales.

camomile-cured salmon with baby spinach, red capsicum salsa and pear and wasabi sauce

serves 4   *Justin Connell* INFLIGHT CHEF ANSETT INTERNATIONAL

The UNUSUAL FLAVOURS are well balanced by the spinach, which cuts the RICH TASTE of the salmon, and the SHARPNESS of the wasabi is MELLOWED by the pear.

salmon

I use camomile-cured salmon from Tasmania for this dish. If it is unavailable, use smoked salmon.

baby spinach leaves, washed and dried
200 g camomile-cured salmon, cut into 16 slices

PEAR AND WASABI SAUCE
2 pears, peeled, halved and cored
2 cups sugar syrup (dissolve equal quantities of water and sugar)
1/2 cup red wine vinegar, Forum Cabernet Sauvignon if available
salt
wasabi

RED CAPSICUM SALSA
1/4 cup red capsicum, diced small
1/4 cup red onion, diced small
1/4 cup tomatoes, peeled and diced small
5 tablespoons extra virgin olive oil, plus extra
1/4 bunch fresh basil leaves, shredded
salt and freshly ground black pepper to taste

To make the pear and wasabi sauce, poach the pears by placing the pear halves in a deep saucepan and covering with hot sugar syrup and silicone paper. Bring almost to the boil and place a plate or lid on top of the paper to prevent the fruit from floating above the surface. Remove the saucepan from the heat and allow the pears to poach slowly until soft. Cool in the cooking liquid, then blend the pears with the wine vinegar and the salt and wasabi to taste. Reserve.

To make the red capsicum salsa, combine all the ingredients in a bowl, season to taste and reserve.

To serve, season and dress the spinach leaves with the extra olive oil. Layer the spinach leaves and salmon slices alternately on the 4 plates. Drizzle the pear and wasabi sauce over and around, and place 5 teaspoons of red capsicum salsa around each plate.

seared calamari with bitter green salad, five-spiced chilli salt, palm sugar and lime dressing

serves 4–6　　　　　*Teage Ezard* EZARD AT ADELPHI MELBOURNE

This DISH relies heavily on the CONTRASTING flavours it delivers – warm, soft CHILLI calamari on a CRISP bed of bitter green SALAD leaves with the underlying FLAVOURS of Chinese FIVE-SPICE powder and LIME juice.

1 kg fresh baby calamari
virgin olive oil

CHILLI SALT
2 tablespoons Maldon
  sea salt flakes
1/4 teaspoon dried
  red chilli flakes
1/4 teaspoon Chinese
  five-spice powder
1/4 teaspoon onion powder
1/4 teaspoon garlic powder

SALAD
1/2 bunch curly cress or
  watercress, picked over,
  washed and dried
1/2 bunch rocket leaves,
  picked over, washed
  and dried
1/4 bunch fresh mint
  leaves, picked over,
  washed and shredded
1/4 bunch fresh coriander
  leaves, picked over,
  washed and shredded
1 Lebanese cucumber,
  peeled, cored and diced
1 red onion, quartered
  and very finely sliced
  diagonally

DRESSING
2 tablespoons lemon juice
2 tablespoons lime juice
3 tablespoons finely
  grated palm sugar
5 tablespoons virgin
  olive oil

Prepare the calamari by removing the head and tentacles and discarding. Pull off and discard the body's mottled skins. Feel inside the body for the cartilage and discard. Wash in plenty of water then cut into bite-sized pieces and refrigerate.

To make the chilli salt, combine the chilli salt ingredients and store in a dry airtight container.

Prepare the salad ingredients and have them ready to be assembled.

To make the dressing, combine the lemon juice and lime juice and add the palm sugar. Check for the balance of flavours and adjust – it needs to be sour to sweet. Add the olive oil and let the dressing stand until needed.

To serve, season the calamari with the chilli salt. Pour some olive oil into a wok or frying pan and over a very high heat cook the calamari until tender, about 1 minute. Toss the salad ingredients with the dressing and add the calamari straight from the wok or pan into the salad so it is served slightly warm. Gently toss the ingredients together and serve immediately.

wine suggestion
Your favourite riesling.

beer suggestion
Cascade Premium Lager.

herb-crusted east coast tuna with artichokes, beans and tomato salad tossed in a wasabi and mustard dressing

serves 4   *Anthony Papp* INFLIGHT CHEF ANSETT INTERNATIONAL

This dish is very POPULAR on our INTERNATIONAL flights.

It is a very LIGHT and EASY dish to make at home.

wine suggestion

Howard Park Riesling has a crisp finish and complements the tuna.

HERB-CRUSTED TUNA
350 g tuna loin, southern
   blue fin if available
2 tablespoons olive oil
1 1/2 tablespoons
   Dijon mustard
1 1/2 tablespoons soy sauce
2 tablespoons fresh
   parsley, chopped
2 tablespoons fresh dill,
   chopped
2 tablespoons fresh
   coriander, chopped

**WASABI AND MUSTARD
DRESSING**
salt and freshly ground
   black pepper
1 teaspoon Dijon mustard
2 egg yolks
wasabi to taste
2 tablespoons white
   wine vinegar
6 tablespoons olive oil
juice 1/4 lemon

SALAD
4 cooked artichoke hearts,
   sliced
12 green beans, cooked
   and split in half
   lengthways
12 butter beans, cooked
   and split in half
   lengthways
8 semi-dried tomato
   halves

To make the herb-crusted tuna, carefully trim all the blood and sinew from the tuna. In a very hot frying pan, heat the olive oil and quickly seal all around the outside of the tuna. Remove from the pan and allow to cool. Mix the mustard and soy sauce together and brush a thin coating on the outside of the tuna. Mix the herbs together in a bowl. Roll the cold tuna in the mixed herbs then in cling wrap, to ensure that the herbs stay on. Rest the tuna for 8 hours in the refrigerator. Slice the tuna into 8 portions and remove the cling wrap after it has been cut (this makes it easier to cut and ensures that the herbs stay on the tuna).

To make the wasabi and mustard dressing, place the salt, pepper, mustard, egg yolks, wasabi and vinegar in a bowl. Whisk until white then add the olive oil slowly, to ensure that the dressing does not split. Finish with the lemon juice and extra salt to taste.

To make the salad, mix all the ingredients in a bowl then add 2 1/2 tablespoons of wasabi and mustard dressing.

To serve, place the salad in 4 deep bowls and put the tuna slices on top. Drizzle the wasabi dressing around the bowl.

saffron spaghetti with crab meat, roasted pimiento, fennel and basil

serves 6   *Christine Manfield* THE PARAMOUNT RESTAURANT SYDNEY

Inspired by the SEDUCTIVE flavours of SPAIN, this EASY-to-PREPARE pasta relies on the ultimate QUALITY of each ingredient, COMBINING to create a real TASTE EXPLOSION.

wine suggestion
Pinot gris or pinot grigio, from Victoria or Tasmania.

500 g spaghetti
2 1/2 tablespoons extra virgin olive oil
1 tablespoon unsalted butter
1 g saffron threads
1 small red onion, finely diced
6 garlic cloves, minced
2 small red chillies, minced
2 ripe tomatoes, peeled and diced
3 tablespoons roasted pimiento strips (Spanish piquillo peppers)
500 g freshly cooked crab meat (South Australian blue swimmer or Queensland mudcrab)
3 tablespoons shaved fennel
1 tablespoon sea salt
1 teaspoon freshly ground black pepper
2 tablespoons extra virgin olive oil
3 tablespoons torn basil leaves

Cook the spaghetti in a large saucepan of lightly salted, boiling water. Heat the olive oil and butter in a heavy-based frying pan and add the saffron threads. Cook over a gentle heat for 1 minute for the colour to infuse into the oil. Add the onion, garlic and chilli and gently sauté for a minute until fragrant, but not coloured. Add the diced tomato, pimiento strips, crab meat and fennel. Toss over the heat to combine. Season with salt and pepper.

Strain the cooked pasta and toss with the olive oil.

To serve, twirl the pasta around a fork and place in the centre of a plate or bowl in a cone shape. Add the crab sauce and garnish with the torn basil leaves.

terrine of salmon with
yabby tails and a salad of fennel

serves 14   *Liam Tomlin* BANC SYDNEY

A DELICATE starter that I like to put on our spring menu. Although the SALMON and YABBY terrine is a time-consuming dish to make, it can be started the day before.

1.5 kg live yabbies, from Pemberton if available

1 x 700 g piece salmon fillet, skin removed

2 medium leeks

6 large tomatoes, peeled, seeded and quartered

salt and freshly ground black pepper

10 g fresh chives, sliced

10 g fresh chervil leaves, chopped

10 g fresh tarragon leaves, chopped

TOMATO CONSOMMÉ

1.6 kg over-ripe egg-shaped (Roma) tomatoes

2 golden shallots, sliced thinly

1 small bunch fresh tarragon, chopped

1 small bunch fresh basil, chopped

1/2 tablespoon white wine

1 teaspoon sugar

1 tablespoon Maldon sea salt

freshly ground black pepper

8 leaves gelatine

POACHING LIQUID

4 cups fish stock

2 1/2 tablespoons Pernod

2 1/2 tablespoons Noilly Prat

stalks reserved from chervil and tarragon

100 g fennel trimmings

6 golden shallots, sliced

pinch saffron threads

salt and freshly ground black pepper

DRESSING FOR TERRINE

5 tablespoons reduced salmon poaching liquid

1 tablespoon champagne vinegar

1 tablespoon Pernod

pinch saffron threads

1/4 cup citrus olive oil

1 1/4 cups extra virgin olive oil

sugar

salt and freshly ground black pepper

lemon juice

GARNISH

4 fennel bulbs, thinly sliced

extra virgin olive oil

salt and freshly ground black pepper

lemon juice

1/2 cup diced tomato, skin and seeds removed

sprigs fresh chervil

To make the tomato consommé, core and roughly chop the tomatoes. Place them in a bowl with the shallots, chopped herbs, wine, sugar, salt and a twist of pepper. Mix all the ingredients together and cover with cling wrap. Place in the refrigerator for 4 hours to allow the flavours to infuse.

Transfer the tomato mixture into a muslin cloth or a clean tea towel and tie tightly. Hang in the refrigerator overnight with a bowl underneath to catch the juices released by the tomatoes. Using a coffee filter paper, decant the tomato consommé into another bowl (to remove any sediment), cover with cling wrap and refrigerate until needed.

Soften the gelatine in cold water and squeeze dry. Heat the tomato consommé and whisk in the gelatine until dissolved. Take off the heat and set aside until needed.

To prepare the yabbies, remove the heads and put the tails on skewers to prevent them curling. Cook in salted, boiling water for 1–1 1/2 minutes, then refresh in iced water. Remove the yabbies from the skewers, then shell and devein them. Lay out on a tray covered with a clean tea towel. Cover with cling wrap and refrigerate until required.

To make the poaching liquid, in a large saucepan add the fish stock, Pernod, Noilly Prat, herb stalks, fennel, shallots and saffron. Lightly season with salt and pepper. Bring to the boil, reduce the heat and simmer for 15 minutes.

To prepare the salmon, cut it into a piece 8.5 cm wide x 26 cm long to fit into a 1.2 litre terrine mould. Any trimmings can be reserved for another dish.

Remove the poaching liquid from the stove. Place the salmon gently into it. Allow the salmon to sit in the liquid as it cools down, poaching slowly so that the centre remains pink. When cool, gently lift the salmon out and place on the tea towel with the yabbies. Cover until required. Pass the poaching liquid through a fine sieve into a clean saucepan, return to the heat and reduce to 5 tablespoons and allow to cool. This will be used later to make the dressing for the terrine.

continued page 146

terrine of salmon
with yabby tails
and a salad of fennel

wine suggestion

A wine that would match this dish would be the 1997 Yeringberg Marsanne, from the Yarra Valley, Victoria.

tip

The tomato consommé for the jelly can be served as a starter – just omit the gelatine. The recipe for the terrine makes 14 portions and cannot really be made in smaller quantities.

To assemble, line the terrine mould with a double layer of cling wrap, pressing it into the corners. Line this with a layer of half the leeks, overlapping each other and pressing well into the corners. The leek should overhang the sides of the terrine by 6 cm each side.

Square the sides of the tomato quarters and lightly season with salt and pepper. Pour $2/3$ cup of tomato jelly into the terrine and allow to set slightly before covering with a layer of tomato quarters, presentation side down.

Lightly season the yabby tails with salt and pepper. Pour another $2/3$ cup of tomato jelly over the tomato quarters and allow to set slightly before adding a layer of yabby tails, closely packed together to cover the entire surface.

Pour another $2/3$ cup of tomato jelly into the terrine to cover the yabbies. Allow it to set slightly before adding a second layer of tomato quarters. Measure out another $2/3$ cup of tomato jelly and add the chives, chervil and tarragon. Pour over the second layer of tomato quarters. Allow to set slightly.

Lightly season the salmon, gently place it into the terrine and cover with the last of the tomato jelly. Allow to set slightly before covering with the remaining leek. Place the terrine in refrigerator for at least 5 hours to set before turning out and cutting.

To make the dressing, place the reduced poaching liquid in a bowl, add the champagne vinegar, Pernod and saffron threads. Stand in a warm area for 15 minutes to allow saffron to infuse. Whisk in the citrus olive oil and extra virgin olive oil. Season to taste with sugar, salt, pepper and lemon juice. If the dressing is too thick, add a little water.

To prepare the fennel, slice the bulbs as thinly as possible – use an electric slicing machine for the best results. Place in a bowl and season to taste with some olive oil, salt, pepper and lemon juice.

Invert the terrine onto a board. If it doesn't slide out easily, run a tea towel under hot water, squeeze out and place onto the terrine to help loosen it. Allow the terrine to stand at room temperature for 10–15 minutes before serving.

To serve, place a 10 cm pastry ring in the centre of each plate and spread a thin layer of fennel inside it. Using a very sharp knife, cut the terrine into 1 cm slices. Lightly season each slice with salt and pepper. Place a slice of terrine on the fennel salad. Spoon the dressing and tomato dice around the terrine. Garnish with chervil.

tranche of Tasmanian Atlantic salmon with soft herb and cheese crust, peperonata, stuffed baby octopus and vine-ripened tomato butter

serves 4   *Marcus Moore* HOTEL SOFITEL MELBOURNE

This is a FAVOURITE recipe of mine that is currently on our MENU in Le Restaurant. Although it LOOKS complicated, it is actually a SIMPLE and TASTY dish which is GREAT in spring or summer, as it is very LIGHT.

12 baby octopus tubes, cleaned

4 x 140 g Tasmanian salmon fillets

olive oil, plus extra for deep-frying

4 baby octopus tentacles, cleaned

4 fresh basil leaves

squeeze lemon juice

TOMATO LEAVES

3 ripe egg-shaped (Roma) tomatoes

sea salt

1 tablespoon fresh thyme leaves

virgin olive oil

2 garlic cloves, thinly sliced

FISH MOUSSE

250 g firm, white fish fillets

1 1/2 cups cream

1 egg white

salt and freshly ground black pepper

pinch cayenne

1 tablespoon freshly chopped dill

PEPERONATA

1 red capsicum

1 green capsicum

2 zucchini

2 finger eggplants

1/2 onion

2 tablespoons virgin olive oil

1 garlic clove

dash Pernod

salt and freshly ground black pepper

TOMATO BUTTER SAUCE

1 punnet ripe cherry tomatoes

2 ripe egg-shaped (Roma) tomatoes

1 teaspoon tomato ketchup

15 g unsalted butter

HERB CRUST

1/3 cup breadcrumbs

1/3 cup grated cheddar cheese

1 tablespoon freshly chopped thyme leaves

3 tablespoons freshly chopped parsley

40 g soft butter

salt and freshly ground black pepper

To prepare the tomato leaves, blanch and peel the tomatoes. Cut them into quarters and remove the seeds. Lay the quarters flat and sprinkle with the sea salt, thyme, olive oil and sliced garlic. Leave in a warm place for 4–6 hours to dehydrate.

To make the fish mousse, pre-chill the food processor bowl in the refrigerator. Blend the fish fillets in the food processor and then pass them through a sieve. In a mixing bowl over ice, add the cream, egg white, salt, pepper, cayenne and dill to the fish.

Place the mixture in a piping bag and pipe into the baby octopus tubes. Seal the tubes with cocktail sticks. Reserve in the refrigerator.

To make the peperonata, cut all vegetables except the garlic into fine brunoise (very small cubes). Heat the olive oil in a frying pan, add the garlic clove and lightly brown. Add the vegetables and sauté over a high heat, keeping them crisp. Add a dash of Pernod and season, then reserve.

To make the tomato butter sauce, purée all the ingredients except the butter and strain through a fine sieve. Reserve – the butter will be added later.

To make the herb crust, blend the breadcrumbs, cheese and thyme in a food processor. Add the parsley and blend until it is a lovely garden green colour. Add the butter and season. Remove the mixture from the food processor and place it on a sheet of silicone paper. Roll it out with a rolling pin to a thickness of 3 mm. Place it in the refrigerator until it is set. Cut into suitable sizes to fit over the salmon fillets.

continued page 148

wine suggestion
1997 Gembrook Hill
Sauvignon Blanc from the
Yarra Valley, Victoria. It is a
ripe, herbaceous style of
sauvignon which marries well
with the herbs and salmon.

tasmania salmon
Tasmanian salmon has a
unique mild flavour that goes
well with the baby octopus
and light cheese crust in
this recipe.

Preheat the oven to 180°C. To assemble the dish, lightly seal the salmon fillets on both sides in a hot oiled frying pan. Cool slightly, then place the herb crust on top of each fillet. Place in the preheated oven for 5–6 minutes.

Place the baby octopus tubes in a steamer, cook lightly for 3–4 minutes then remove the cocktail sticks. Deep-fry the octopus tentacles and the basil leaves in olive oil in a hot frying pan, then sprinkle with the lemon juice.

To serve, place the tomato leaves on top of the steamed baby octopus tubes and place them at the head of each plate. Place the peperonata in the centre, and put the salmon fillets below the peperonata. Top the peperonata with the octopus tentacles and basil leaves. Stir the remaining butter into the tomato butter sauce and warm through. Pour it around each plate.

tranche of
Tasmanian Atlantic
salmon with soft
herb and cheese
crust, peperonata,
stuffed baby
octopus and vine-
ripened tomato
butter

roasted new season Barossa lamb with pissaladière tart, broad beans and extra virgin olive oil sauce

serves 4   *Paul Wilson* RADII RESTAURANT & BAR PARK HYATT MELBOURNE

A very informal GOURMET experience which I think typifies the BEAUTY of eating and COOKING here in Australia. Carve the LAMB at the table and serve with slices of the FRESHLY baked tart and a CHILLED South Australian riesling.

main

juice 2 lemons

$1/2$ cup extra virgin olive oil, Joseph from South Australia if available

2 garlic cloves, split and crushed

1 teaspoon sea salt

1 teaspoon freshly cracked black pepper

1.5 kg leg milk-fed spring lamb, from Barossa Valley, South Australia if available

12 fillets good quality anchovies, from Mendosa, Western Australia if available

2 tablespoons small black niçoise olives, pitted

4 tablespoons white wine

1 carrot, cut into 12 mm dice

1 onion, cut into 12 mm dice

1 celery stick, cut into 12 mm dice

1 garlic clove, cut into 12 mm dice

2 cups reduced lamb stock

$1/4$ cup basil stalks

$1/2$ cup broad beans, podded and cooked just before serving

$1/4$ cup basil leaves

PISSALADIÈRE DOUGH

$1 1/4$ cups warm water

1 sachet dry yeast

1 cup rye flour

$1 1/3$ cups warm water

3 tablespoons milk

$1/2$ cup olive oil, plus a little extra

1 teaspoon salt

1 cup plain flour

CARAMELISED ONIONS

30 g unsalted butter

8 brown onions, peeled and finely sliced

1 garlic clove, finely sliced

salt and freshly ground black pepper

6 teaspoons brown sugar

1 tablespoon red wine vinegar

1 teaspoon thyme leaves

$1 1/2$ tablespoons reduced lamb stock

To make the pissaladière dough, combine the warm water, dry yeast and rye flour in a large mixing bowl. Allow to rise, covered with a clean tea towel, in a warm place for 20 minutes. Then add the warm water, milk, olive oil, salt and plain flour. Knead all the ingredients together for 5–6 minutes. Roll the dough into a clean bowl which has been brushed with olive oil. Allow to rise for 2 hours in a warm place. Knead well, then let it prove for a further 40 minutes. Store in a cool place.

To make the caramelised onions, place the butter in a frying pan over a medium heat. Add the sliced onions, garlic and season with salt and pepper. Mix together then turn the heat down and cook gently until the onions soften and begin to brown. Add the brown sugar and continue to cook the onions until they caramelise. Then add the red wine vinegar and reduce completely. Add the thyme and stock and cook slowly for 25 minutes, until the onions have formed a soft, dry marmalade consistency. Reserve.

Preheat the oven to 180°C.

To roast the lamb, combine the lemon juice, half the olive oil, garlic, salt and pepper. Pour the mixture over the leg of lamb, rubbing it well into the lamb. Allow to marinate briefly – for 15 minutes. Place the lamb into a baking pan and roast in the preheated oven for 20 minutes for medium rare and 35 minutes for well-cooked lamb. Baste throughout the cooking process. Very small legs of milk-fed spring lamb cook very fast.

While the lamb is cooking, make the pissaladière tarts. Roll out the dough to 2 x 1 cm thick sheets. Cut into 25 cm diameter disks and place on oiled pie or pizza oven sheets (1 tart equals 2 serves). Spread the bases with the caramelised onion, leaving a 1 cm border around the edge. Arrange the anchovy fillets in a criss-cross fashion on top of the onion, allowing 6 fillets per tart. Dot with the olives and bake in the oven for the last 5 minutes of the lamb's cooking time. Once the lamb and the tarts are cooked, keep them all warm while you make the sauce.

continued page 152

wine suggestion

Serve with Leo Buring's
Leonay Riesling, Eden.

simple diversity

This very simple dish reflects
the diversity of Australia's
excellent food – the Western
Australian anchovies in the
sweet and salty pissaladière
tart, the milk-fed lamb from
the Barossa married with the
first broad bean harvest from
Victoria, and the delicate
sauce made from extra virgin
olive oil from South Australia.

Remove the lamb from the baking pan and pour white wine
into the pan. Place it over a high heat, add the diced vegetables
and cook until the wine has reduced by half. Add the lamb stock
and basil stalks, bring to the boil and then pass through a fine
sieve. Place sauce in a saucepan over a high heat and bring to
the boil.

To serve, carve the lamb and place it on 4 warm serving plates.
Scatter the broad beans and basil leaves over the top. Whisk
the remaining olive oil into the boiling lamb sauce. Spoon it
generously over the lamb and serve immediately with half a warm
pissaladière tart.

roasted new season
Barossa lamb
with pissaladière
tart, broad beans
and extra virgin
olive oil sauce

spring lamb with
a goat's cheese
soufflé, and green
pea coulis with
parsnip and red
capsicum

spring lamb with a goat's cheese soufflé, and green pea coulis with parsnip and red capsicum

serves 6   *Werner Kimmeringer* NATIONAL EXECUTIVE CHEF ANSETT

Make this dish in SPRING when the grass is green, the lamb is small, and the lamb FLAVOUR not so developed. Goat's milk is also RICHER now so CHEESE makers can produce their FINEST.

main

3 lamb rumps

finely cracked black pepper

4 cloves garlic,
   freshly crushed

2 branches rosemary

olive oil

6 x 50 g spring lamb
   cutlets, trimmed

90 g fresh green peas,
   blanched and kept hot

15 g fresh butter, melted

6 tablespoons strong
   lamb stock, hot

BECHAMEL SAUCE

1/2 cup milk

1 tablespoon butter

1 tablespoon flour

GOAT'S CHEESE SOUFFLÉ

2 egg yolks

salt and finely cracked
   black pepper

50 g parmesan cheese,
   freshly grated

75 g crumbled semihard
   goat's cheese, Chevrotin
   Faudel if available

60 g egg whites

1 1/2 tablespoons lemon
   juice

5 g butter

1/4 cup hazelnuts, toasted
   and ground

GREEN PEA COULIS

3 golden shallots,
   finely chopped

1 garlic clove,
   finely chopped

1 1/2 tablespoons olive oil

1/4 cup green split peas,
   soaked overnight
   and drained

1/2 teaspoon freshly grated
   nutmeg

1 teaspoon finely cracked
   black pepper

1 teaspoon salt

1 1/2 cups vegetable stock

50 g fresh peas

20 g spinach leaves,
   blanched

2 1/2 tablespoons
   fresh cream

**PARSNIP AND RED
CAPSICUM**

3 medium parsnips, washed
   and peeled

1 large red capsicum
   (even sides are better for
   cutting), washed

1 1/2 tablespoons olive oil

1 tablespoon freshly
   chopped thyme leaves

1 tablespoon freshly
   chopped flat-leafed
   parsley

1/2 garlic clove, chopped

salt and freshly ground
   black pepper to taste

To make the bechamel sauce, boil the milk and let stand for 5 minutes. Melt the butter over a medium heat, mix the flour in with a wooden spoon to form a roux. Add the milk, a little at a time and continue stirring until the sauce has thickened. Allow to cool.

Preheat the oven to 180°C.

To make the goat's cheese soufflé, mix the egg yolks, seasoning, parmesan cheese and the goat's cheese with the bechamel sauce. Whip the egg whites with the lemon juice to a semihard stage and fold carefully into the cheese mix.

Butter small moulds or expresso cups with a little butter, sprinkle with the toasted ground hazelnuts then add the cheese mix. Place the cups in a shallow water bath of simmering water and cook in the oven for 15 minutes. Reserve. They will be double baked.

To make the pea coulis, in a heavy-based saucepan, sweat the shallots and garlic in the olive oil, add the split peas, the seasonings and the vegetable stock and simmer until soft. Add the fresh peas and the spinach and when the leaves are wilted, remove from the heat and purée in the blender or food processor. Pass it through a fine sieve, add the cream and put it in a saucepan over a low heat. Bring it to the boil, check the seasoning and reserve in a warm place.

Preheat the oven to 230°C.

wine suggestion

My first choice of wine would
be a strong pinot noir such
as 1998 Yarra Ridge from the
Yarra Valley in Victoria. A
cabernet franc would also be
a perfect match for the lamb.

beer suggestion

Cascade Premium Lager.

To cook the parsnip and red capsicum, cut each parsnip into
6 pieces lengthways. Cut off the centre core of each wedge.
Cut the top off the red capsicum, remove the seeds and cut into
12 triangles. Remove all the soft parts from the flesh. Season the
parsnip and red capsicum with the olive oil, herbs, garlic, salt and
pepper, and bake in the preheated oven until the parsnip is
golden and the capsicum starts to have dark edges, about 10–15
minutes. Reserve in a warm place.

Reduce the oven temperature to 180°C.

To cook the lamb rumps, season with the pepper, half the garlic
and rosemary and bake on an oiled baking tray in the oven for
15–20 minutes, until pink. Reserve and rest in a warm place.

To pan-fry the lamb cutlets, season with pepper and the
remaining garlic and rosemary and seal both sides in a hot oiled
frying pan. Place them next to the rump in the oven when there are
5–7 minutes left to cook.

To heat the fresh green peas, blanch them in boiling salted water
for 5 seconds and refresh them under cold water. When needed,
toss them in the melted butter, season and serve immediately.

To serve, reheat the goat's cheese soufflé in the hot oven for
5 minutes. Carve the lamb rumps into 6 slices, and fold 3 slices over
each of the lamb cutlets. Place some green pea coulis on each warm
plate, arrange the baked vegetables and the green peas on top and
place the lamb cutlets on it to gain height on the plate. Place the
soufflé beside it or leave in the cup if it matches the plate. Spoon the
strong hot lamb juice over the meat.

Port Phillip Bay garfish with wild olives, potatoes, mint and watercress

serves 4   *Trevor Bilney* BALI INTER-CONTINENTAL RESORT ON JIMBARAN BEACH

I LOVE fishing for garfish. The taste is very SPECIAL: pure and REFINED. Although garfish is not exclusive to Australian waters, our VARIETY is perfect. The bottle filleting technique is a NEAT trick used by the OLDTIMERS who hang out at the pier.

wine suggestion

Try Stonier's Chardonnay or Red Hill Estate Champagne, both from the Mornington Peninsula, Victoria.

8 whole garfish
olive oil
5 tablespoons dry sherry
24 wild olives, stones removed, from Adelaide Hills if available
fresh lemon thyme twigs
salt and freshly ground black pepper
4 kipfler potatoes, thickly sliced, from Dobson Farm if available

WATERCRESS SALAD
1/3 cup raisins, chopped
juice 2 lemons
2 tablespoons olive oil
2 tablespoons pinenuts
salt and freshly ground black pepper
1/2 cup fresh mint leaves, from Omeo if available
4 cups watercress tips

Preheat the oven to 200°C.

To prepare the garfish, gut the fish and hold it down on its back. Press on the back bone with an empty bottle, right along the length of the cavity opening – basically from head to tail. This method will release the backbone at the head and remove it to where the intestines finish. Then remove the ribs with a filleting knife.

Lay the garfish on an oiled baking tray and sprinkle with the sherry. Add the olives and lemon thyme and season with salt and pepper. Bake in the preheated oven for 11 minutes.

At the same time, sauté the potatoes until crispy in 3 tablespoons of hot olive oil in a large frying pan.

To make the watercress salad, soak the raisins in a bowl with the lemon juice and the olive oil. Dry roast the pinenuts in a non-stick frying pan over a medium heat, stirring, until golden. When ready to serve, add the pinenuts to the salad and season to taste with salt and pepper. Add the mint and watercress leaves and gently combine.

To serve, place some salad on each serving plate with some potatoes alongside. Top the salad with 2 garfish (per serve), and arrange the olives and lemon thyme on top. Sprinkle any leftover juice from the fish around the plate.

main

red date and tomato curry of Geraldton scallops

serves 4   *Gary Jones* JONES RESTAURANT SUBIACO

An AROMATIC coconut sauce blended with the FLAVOURS of tomatoes, capsicums and dates makes a PERFECT marriage with the FRESH sea TASTE of the scallops.

2 kg (about 24) fresh scallops in shell, from Geraldton if available
a little oil

CURRY PASTE

4 tablespoons canola oil
2 stalks lemongrass (tender part only), finely chopped
3 tomatoes, peeled and seeded
3 garlic cloves, chopped
1 tablespoon chopped ginger
2 red chillies
2 tablespoons chopped fresh coriander leaves

SAUCE

4 tablespoons canola oil
1 red capsicum, cut into 1 cm dice
1 green capsicum, cut into 1 cm dice
1 punnet cherry tomatoes, peeled, seeded and diced
2 1/2 cups coconut cream
1 1/4 cups coconut water, from young coconuts
5 tablespoons fish sauce
1 tablespoon fresh coriander leaves
150 g red dates, presoaked, diced and stoned
juice 2 limes
2 spring onions, sliced diagonally
1/3 cup palm sugar

To make the curry paste, blend all the ingredients together in a food processor or blender until it is a fine paste.

To make the sauce, put the canola oil in a large saucepan and sweat the capsicum for a few minutes. Add the tomatoes, and sweat for 2 minutes. Add the curry paste, coconut cream and coconut water, and reduce the liquid by half. Add the fish sauce, coriander, dates, lime juice and spring onions and mix together. Bring back to the boil and finish with the palm sugar. Remove from the heat when thickened to a sauce consistency.

Clean and remove the scallops from their shells. Quickly cook the scallops in a hot oiled frying pan, searing on both sides for about 1 minute, until just opaque.

To serve, place equal amounts of scallops on 4 scallop shells which are sitting on 4 serving plates. Coat liberally with the sauce.

main

lamb shanks braised in Asian spices

serves 4   *Michael Mangan* PARKROYAL HOTEL KUALA LUMPUR

This RECIPE is actually based on a pork recipe that I have ADAPTED here in Malaysia called BAK KUT TEH, which means 'pork cooked in tea'. The AROMA from the SPICES is wonderful.

main

2 tablespoons peanut oil
1/4 cup water
4 baby pak choy, washed
and trimmed

LAMB BRAISE
4 lamb shanks
(ask your butcher
to French trim them)
seasoned flour
2 tablespoons peanut oil
4 garlic cloves
4 cups chicken stock
1 1/2 tablespoons red wine
vinegar
1 1/2 tablespoons oyster
sauce
2 teaspoons dark soy sauce
1 teaspoon hoisin sauce
1 teaspoon crushed
Szechuan pepper
1 star anise
1 cinnamon stick
1 clove
1 teaspoon cornflour

CHOW MEIN
200 g fine fresh yellow
Chinese noodles
1 tablespoon peanut oil
1 red capsicum, diced
50 g fresh mushrooms,
sliced
2 garlic cloves, crushed
2 teaspoons soy sauce
2 teaspoons oyster sauce
2 teaspoons Chinese chilli
sauce
1 1/2 tablespoons sherry
1 cup chicken stock
2 teaspoons white wine
vinegar
1 teaspoon sugar
4 spring onions, sliced
diagonally

wine suggestion
My favourite wine with this is a pinot noir, preferably from Wantirna Estate, Yarra Valley, Victoria.

Preheat the oven to 180°C.

To cook the lamb, dust the shanks lightly in seasoned flour. Heat the peanut oil in a braising pan and when the oil is hot, brown the lamb all over then add the garlic and fry a little. Add all the remaining lamb braise ingredients except the cornflour. Bring to the boil, cover and transfer to the oven. Gently braise for about 1 1/2 hours or until tender. Test by inserting a small knife into the meat.

Remove the shanks from the stock, and place them in a warmed serving dish. Keep in a warm place.

Strain the stock into a saucepan, bring to the boil, skimming off any excess fat from the top. Mix the cornflour with a little water to form a light paste and add it slowly to the simmering sauce while whisking until it is a nice consistency. Pour the sauce over the shanks.

To make the chow mein, boil some water in a large saucepan and cook the noodles for 2 minutes and drain. While they are draining, put the peanut oil in a wok or frying pan and stir-fry the capsicum, mushrooms and garlic. Add the sauces, sherry, stock, vinegar and sugar. Bring to the boil, reduce the liquid by half and add the blanched noodles, stirring well. Top with the spring onions.

Just before serving, cook the pak choy. Heat a wok over a medium heat and add the peanut oil, then the water. When it is hot, stir-fry the pak choy until it is just beginning to wilt.

To serve, place a lamb shank on each serving plate and pour some sauce over it. Place the chow mein noodles next to the lamb and garnish the lamb with sautéed pak choy.

160 dining high

Koonawarra kid with toasted fontina cake and crisp greens

serves 8   *Gary Cooper* ELEONORE'S RESTAURANT CHÂTEAU YERING YARRA VALLEY

TENDER kid goat's meat with TUSCAN tomato, garlic and rosemary with white wine vinegar OVERTONES.

wine suggestion
1996 Mount Mary Cabernet.

4 kg kid's meat (from the Yarra Valley if available), boned, trimmed and cut into 4 cm cubes
salt and freshly ground black pepper
2 cups virgin olive oil
10 large onions, finely sliced
2 teaspoons chilli paste
2 cups white wine vinegar
6 cups dry white wine
1 bunch rosemary
3 heads garlic, unpeeled
4 cups beef stock
6 cups tomato concasse (tomatoes, peeled, seeds removed and diced)
1 1/4 cups tomato paste
48 green beans, topped and tailed
1/2 cup almond slivers, toasted
1/2 cup finely chopped fresh parsley

FONTINA CAKE
6 potatoes, sliced thinly
80 g blue cheese, crumbled
150 g fontina cheese, grated
200 g clarified butter

To cook the meat, season it and heat the oil in a saucepan over a high heat to a smoking temperature. Add about a third of the meat and brown well all over. It is important to keep the cooking temperature very high. Do not add too much meat at once as this will lower the temperature and the meat will stew rather than brown. Remove the meat with a slotted spoon. Add more oil as necessary. Bring the oil back to the heat again and repeat the process until all the meat has been browned. Reserve the meat.

Reduce the heat and add the onions and chilli paste. Do not let the onions brown. Stir and scrape off all the bits clinging to the bottom of the saucepan. When the onions are translucent, add the vinegar and wine. Increase the heat to a slow simmer and reduce the liquid by half. This takes about half an hour.

Add the meat, rosemary, garlic, stock, tomato concasse, tomato paste and salt and pepper and gently mix. Cover and cook until the meat is soft, about 1 1/2 hours. Adjust the seasoning.

Preheat the oven to 180°C.

To make the fontina cake, line a gratin dish with buttered silicone paper. Layer the potatoes, blue cheese, fontina cheese and clarified butter 4–5 layers high. Bake in the oven until the potato is cooked and golden on top, about 15–20 minutes. Remove from the oven and when cold cut with a 5 cm pastry cutter into rounds or slice into wedges. Heat up in the oven just before serving.

To serve, blanch the beans in boiling water, drain and place 6 on each plate, garnished with the toasted almonds. Place some meat and its sauce on each plate and garnish with the chopped parsley. A wedge or round of fontina cake completes the plating.

'Kreem-b-tween' of honeycomb ice cream with florentines

serves 4

Andrew Blake BLAKES RESTAURANT MELBOURNE

I remember as a CHILD unwrapping a small block of VANILLA ICE CREAM and sandwiching it between two WAFER biscuits. This dish is less ceremonial but equally ENJOYABLE.

wine suggestion
Mt Horrocks Cordon Cut Riesling.

FLORENTINES
30 g unsalted butter
2 teaspoons thickened cream
6 teaspoons sugar
1/3 cup flaked almonds
1 1/2 teaspoons cherries, finely diced
1 teaspoon mixed peel
40 g dark chocolate
1 sheet gold leaf (optional)

ICE CREAM
6 egg yolks
1/2 cup sugar
2 cups thickened cream
3/4 cup milk
100 ml cup leatherwood honey
100 g honeycomb, chopped, plus extra (optional)

CARAMEL SAUCE
2 1/2 tablespoons sugar
2 1/2 tablespoons water
4 tablespoons cream

Preheat the oven to 175°C.

To make the florentines, melt the butter, cream and sugar together in a saucepan over a low heat, stirring constantly until thick and creamy. Remove from the heat and stir in the almonds, cherries and peel. Place teaspoonfuls of the mixture onto baking sheets lined with baking paper. Flatten out the mixture slightly with a wet spoon and leave plenty of space between each biscuit for expansion. Bake in the preheated oven until golden brown, about 8–10 minutes. Lift the florentines off the sheets with a metal spatula and let them cool on a baking rack.

Melt the dark chocolate in a bowl sitting in a pan of simmering water and beat until smooth. Put it in an icing bag with a small nozzle and pipe it in a squiggle formation on the rough side of half of the florentines. Divide the gold leaf, if liked, among the florentines and let it fall onto the chocolate.

To make the ice cream, beat the egg yolks and sugar on high for 15 minutes, until the mixture is light and fluffy. Meanwhile, bring the cream and milk to a rapid boil. Then whisk in the egg and sugar mixture. Remove from the heat and pour it into a bowl. Add the honey to taste. Let the custard cool, then churn in an ice cream maker according to the manufacturer's instructions. Stir in the chopped honeycomb and freeze in a tray to a depth of 3 cm.

To make the caramel sauce, make a caramel by putting the sugar and water in a saucepan over a high heat. When it is golden, cool it by stirring in the cream. Remove immediately from the heat.

To serve, drizzle some caramel sauce in a zigzag pattern on each of the serving plates. Place a plain florentine on each plate. Top with a 5 cm square or round of the ice cream and place a chocolate florentine over the ice cream. Serve with a few shards of honeycomb, if liked.

dessert

rhubarb crostata with pecans

serves 8–10   *John Torode* SMITHS OF SMITHFIELD LONDON

This recipe is very AUSTRALIAN – it reminds me of the fruit and vegetable GARDEN of my CHILDHOOD and swapping RHUBARB and PASSIONFRUIT with the neighbours. I learnt this recipe from a second-generation Australian whose family had come from ITALY many years before.

wine suggestion
Brown Brothers Muscat.

tip
You need to begin cooking the day before serving.

1 1/4 cups soft brown sugar
2 cups King Island cream
poached rhubarb
   (optional)

RHUBARB
250 g rhubarb, cleaned
   and cut into 10 cm
   lengths
3/4 cup sugar
2 vanilla beans
1 tablespoon water

PASTRY
4 cups plain flour
1/4 cup sugar
1/4 teaspoon salt
1 cup finely chopped
   pecans
125 g butter
5 egg yolks
1/2 cup water

RHUBARB PECAN FILLING
1 cup thick cream
1/3 cup sugar
3 1/2 cups pecans, toasted
   and finely chopped

To cook the rhubarb, begin the day before. Preheat the oven to 180°C. Place the rhubarb stems in a baking dish and sprinkle the sugar over. Add the vanilla beans and the water. Cover the dish securely with foil and place the dish in the preheated oven. Reduce the heat to 160°C and leave to cook for 20 minutes. Remove the dish from the oven and leave to cool. Leave the foil well secured – don't even be tempted to look at it.

To make the pastry, rub the flour, sugar, salt, pecan nuts and butter together to the consistency of breadcrumbs. Make a well in the centre and add the egg yolks and water and mix to make a dough. The dough can also be made in a food processor. Once the mixture is at the dough stage, knead for 2 minutes. Cover with cling wrap and leave to rest in the refrigerator overnight.

To make the filling, mix the cream and sugar in a bowl. Add the cooked rhubarb and its juice and then the pecans. Leave the rhubarb cream to chill overnight.

The next day, preheat the oven to 200°C. Roll the dough out to fit a large pie pan about 30 cm square, leaving plenty of dough along the sides. (An alternative is to make individual tarts in 10 cm tart tins.) Pour the rhubarb filling into the centre and pull the dough over the edge of the filling so that it stays in place and the dish is watertight. Sprinkle the filling with the brown sugar and place in the preheated oven. Cook for 35–40 minutes, until the filling is still wobbly and the dough is the consistency of doughnuts.

To serve, place a warm slice on individual plates with a scoop of King Island cream and a few pieces of poached rhubarb, if liked.

dessert

pink grapefruit and
navel orange terrine with blood orange sorbet

serves 6

Peter Doyle CICADA SYDNEY

A DRAMATIC-looking DESSERT of reds, pinks and oranges.
SERVE it with a little PASSIONFRUIT sauce and a glass
BISCUIT, if liked.

wine suggestion
1998 T'Gallant Triumph
Botrytis Pinot Gris,
Mornington, Victoria.

BLOOD ORANGE SORBET
1 cup blood orange juice,
strained
2/3 cup sugar syrup
(dissolve equal
quantities of sugar
and water)

TERRINE
4 pink grapefruit,
segmented
4 navel oranges,
segmented
3 1/2 gelatine leaves
1 cup fresh orange juice,
strained
1 cup sugar syrup
(see above)
1 banana, peeled, cut
into 3 cm lengths
5 strawberries

To make the sorbet, mix the blood orange juice and the sugar syrup together and place in an ice cream maker. Churn according to the manufacturer's instructions.

To make the terrine, remove all the pith from the orange and grapefruit segments. Place them on dry, clean tea towels to soak up excess juices and then chill for 2 hours.

Wrap cling wrap around the bottom of 6 x 80 mm diameter rings. Wrap it tightly around the outside edges of the rings to prevent any juices draining away. An elastic band will help keep the plastic in place.

To make the jelly, soak and submerge the gelatine leaves in water for at least 5 minutes. Mix the orange juice and sugar syrup together. Pour 1 cup of the juice mixture into a small stainless steel saucepan and bring to the boil. Squeeze out the gelatine leaves and whisk them into the hot juice. Dissolve them well. Add the remaining juice and whisk together – pour the mixture into a stainless steel bowl, place the bowl over a bigger bowl of iced water and whisk gently to help chill the jelly. When the jelly is becoming cold and just beginning to take on some viscosity, pour a thin layer into the bottom of each ring (which has been previously lined with cling wrap). Place some segments of grapefruit and orange in the ring. A round of banana can be cut 3 cm high and placed in the centre of each ring and the citrus and sliced strawberries placed around the banana. Pour in some jelly to surround the fruit. Alternate the fruit and jelly to about 3 cm in height. Finish with a layer of jelly and place in the refrigerator for at least 3 hours to set.

To serve, place the jelly rings in the centre of each serving plate and use a blow torch to help ease off the metal rings. Place a scoop of blood orange sorbet in the centre of each jelly and serve immediately.

dessert

strawberries sautéed with shiraz

serves 4–6   *Tony Bilson* AMPERSAND RESTAURANT SYDNEY

A perfect MARRIAGE of tender spring strawberries, SPICES,
crème de cassis and Barossa Valley SHIRAZ. Choose small,
RIPE STRAWBERRIES – try to avoid large ones unless they
are TENDER and have COLOUR all through their flesh.

wine suggestion
Seppelt's Sparkling Shiraz.

SHIRAZ SYRUP
$1^1/_3$ cup Barossa Valley
    shiraz
4 tablespoons caster sugar
$1/_2$ vanilla bean,
    split lengthwise
6 cm piece cinnamon bark
1 star anise

1 orange
5 tablespoons crème de
    cassis
3 tablespoons virgin
    olive oil
3 punnets strawberries,
    hulled, large ones cut
    into quarters
4–6 sponge biscuits
    (langues du chat) or
    sweet biscuits of choice
$1/_2$ cup whipped cream
2 tablespoons icing sugar
    (optional)

To make the shiraz syrup, place all the ingredients in a medium-sized saucepan and bring to the boil. Simmer for 15 minutes and then strain. Take $3/_4$ cup of the syrup, place it in a bowl and chill. Reserve the rest to sauté the strawberries.

Remove the zest of the orange with a vegetable peeler, making sure no pith is attached. Julienne the zest. Blanch the zest in boiling water for 3 minutes. Reserve half the zest, and add the rest to the cassis in a small saucepan. Simmer for 5 minutes. Add the remaining zest and the zest and cassis mixture to the chilled shiraz syrup and keep cold.

Place about 5 tablespoons of the syrup, along with the olive oil, in a large frying pan and bring to the boil over a high heat. Add the strawberries and toss in the syrup over the heat until they begin to soften and are coated with the reduced syrup. Take the cold syrup from the refrigerator and tip the cooked berries from the pan into the cold syrup to arrest their cooking.

To serve, keep the strawberries at room temperature and distribute on the serving plates. Put a sponge biscuit to the side of the strawberries and a spoonful of whipped cream. Dust lightly with icing sugar, if liked.

dessert

Star Alliance Chefs

The Star Alliance network – Air Canada, Air New Zealand, All Nippon Airways, Lufthansa, Scandinavian Airlines, Thai Airways, United Airlines and Varig – is the largest airline network in the world offering travellers unparalleled services right around the world.

Canadian maple syrup mousse with vanilla and raspberry sauce

serves 6   *Robert Volstuben* AIR CANADA

24 golden raisins
6 circles of sponge cake, cut to fit foil cups
$1/2$ cup raspberry sauce
$1/2$ cup vanilla sauce

MAPLE SYRUP MOUSSE
4 gelatine leaves
$1/4$ cup Canadian maple syrup
1 cup cream (35% fat)
2 teaspoons vanilla sugar
1 tablespoon sugar

To prepare the mousse, soak the gelatine leaves in cold water for 5 minutes. Warm the maple syrup and add the soaked gelatine leaves, stirring constantly until the leaves are dissolved. Whip the cream and gently fold in the sugars. Slowly mix in the maple syrup and gelatine mix, ensuring that the mixture is well incorporated. Place the mousse mixture in a pastry bag and fill 6 small foil cups (about $1/2$ cup). Add 4 raisins to each cup and top with a circle of sponge cake. Chill for 4–6 hours until set.

To serve, briefly dip each foil cup into hot water (5 seconds) to unmould. Place in the centre of the plate, and serve accompanied by raspberry and vanilla sauces.

pictured top

mild chilli-glazed papaya and avocado parcels with exotic herb salad

serves 6   *Huka Lodge* AIR NEW ZEALAND

12 x 20 g slices avocado
12 x 20 g slices papaya
12 rice paper wrappers, soaked in warm water until softened
60 g cellophane noodles, soaked in warm water until softened
1 tablespoon snowpea shoots

CHILLI DRESSING
$1^1/2$ large red chilli, seeded and chopped finely
$1/4$ red capsicum, seeded and chopped finely
$1^1/2$ medium cloves garlic, finely chopped
$1/2$ teaspoon sea salt, Maldon if available
60 g palm sugar
$1^1/2$ tablespoons freshly squeezed lime juice
3 tablespoons Thai fish sauce
3 tablespoons sake or sauvignon blanc

HERB SALAD
6 tablespoons fresh coriander, chopped
6 tablespoons fresh mint, chopped
6 tablespoons fresh Thai basil, chopped
6 tablespoons cucumber, seeded and shredded
6 tablespoons spring onion (white part only), finely sliced
3 tablespoons lemongrass heart, shredded

To make the chilli dressing, place the chilli, capsicum, garlic and sea salt in a mortar and crush finely using a pestle. Add the palm sugar and crush to a paste. Add the lime juice, fish sauce and sake and stir well.

To make the herb salad, mix herbs with cucumber, spring onions and lemongrass heart, and toss with a little of the chilli dressing.

Glaze papaya and avocado with a little chilli dressing and place on the edge of a softened rice paper wrapper. Place noodles and snowpea shoots on top and moisten again with dressing. Roll up and store under a slightly damp tea towel until ready to serve.

Serve papaya and avocado parcels with herb salad and any leftover chilli dressing.

pictured bottom

Pages 172-173: The Twelve Apostles on the Great Ocean Road, Victoria.

175

sukiyaki

serves 4   *Mr Yajima* ALL NIPPON AIRWAYS

- 2 cups dashi soup
- $1/2$ cup sake
- $1/2$ cup mirin
- 600 g extra thin sliced sirloin
- 1 onion, sliced
- 1 leek, washed and sliced
- $1/2$ cup shiitake mushrooms, sliced
- $1/2$ cup Chinese cabbage, shredded
- 1 cup tofu, cut into small pieces
- $1/2$ cup shirataki-kon'nyaku, if available
- $1/2$ cup soy sauce, plus extra
- 5 tablespoons sugar, plus extra

Simmer all ingredients in a heavy-based saucepan at the table. Adjust to taste by adding extra soy sauce (salty) or sugar (sweet). If desired, a beaten raw egg can be added to each bowl.

pictured left

Eifel-style venison sauerbraten

serves 4   *Thomas Stets* LUFTHANSA

This dish goes particularly well with savoy cabbage, cranberries and braised apple, or with different kinds of German dumplings, red cabbage or brussels sprouts.

- 1 kg venison (shoulder or leg)
- salt and freshly ground black pepper
- 3 tablespoons olive oil
- 1 tablespoon tomato paste
- 2 tablespoons sugar beet syrup
- 2 tablespoons apple cider
- 2 slices black bread breadcrumbs
- 1 tablespoon cornflour

MARINADE
- 1 carrot, diced
- 1 celery stalk, diced
- 2 onions, diced
- 1 bottle pinot noir
- $1/3$ cup red wine vinegar
- 1 tablespoon black peppercorns
- 1 tablespoon mustard seeds
- freshly ground black pepper
- 1 tablespoon juniper berries
- 2 bay leaves
- 1 clove
- 1 sprig thyme
- 2 cloves garlic

To make the marinade, combine all of the ingredients in a large bowl. Pour the marinade over the venison and leave to marinate for 7 days in the refrigerator.

On day 8, remove the meat, strain the marinade and save both the marinade and the marinated vegetables. Season the venison with salt and freshly ground black pepper. Pan sear in olive oil before adding the marinated vegetables. When nicely browned, add tomato paste, sugar beet syrup, apple cider and breadcrumbs. Slowly add the marinade and simmer for about 1 $1/2$ to 2 hours, until meat is tender. Remove the meat and reduce the sauce. Thicken the sauce with the cornflour and strain. Return the meat to the sauce to keep warm.

pictured right

grilled fillet of veal in pepper gravy, with lobster tail, glacéed onion, leek, potatoes and green peas

serves 4   *Severin Sjöstedt* SCANDINAVIAN AIRLINES

4 small onions
2 tablespoons sea salt
1 tablespoon raw sugar
4 x 150 g veal fillet
1 leek, thinly sliced
60 g fresh green peas
4–6 large potatoes, cooked and cut into wedges
25 g butter
salt, to taste
2 large lobster tails, cooked and cut lengthways

PEPPER GRAVY
butter for frying
1 duck or chicken carcass
1 carrot, diced
1 onion, diced
1 leek, thinly sliced
1–2 garlic cloves, peeled and coarsely chopped
3–4 bay leaves
3–4 sprigs of thyme
1 teaspoon white peppercorns
1 tablespoon butter
salt, to taste

To make the pepper gravy, melt the butter in a heavy-based saucepan. Chop up the duck or chicken carcass and brown the pieces in the melted butter. Add the diced carrot, onion, leek and garlic, the bay leaves and thyme and pour in just enough water to cover (about 1–1/2 litres). Simmer for approximately 3 hours, skimming occasionally. The liquid should reduce to about one-third. Strain the stock and continue to simmer until reduced to approximately 400 ml. Transfer to a blender. Add white peppercorns and butter and blend. Season with a little salt and strain through a fine sieve. Keep warm until ready to serve.

To prepare the onions, first preheat the oven to 200°C. Place the onions in an ovenproof dish with the sea salt. Brush the onions with some of the pepper gravy and sprinkle the raw sugar on top. Bake for 20–30 minutes, until brown and soft.

Meanwhile, grill the veal on high for 3–4 minutes each side and then set aside to rest.

Blanch the leek and the green peas for a few minutes. Drain, and add the boiled potato wedges and butter. Season with salt and keep warm.

Reduce oven to 120°C and put the veal in the oven for the last 8–10 minutes of the onions' cooking time.

Place the pepper gravy on the plate followed by the veal and the vegetables. Top with a gently warmed quarter of the cooked lobster tail.

pictured left

som tum

serves 4 (as a side salad)   THAI AIRWAYS

Raw papaya can sometimes be difficult to obtain, but the salad works equally well with carrot, cabbage or cucumber.

2 cups raw papaya, shredded
8 bird's eye chillies, bruised (optional)
4 tablespoons of unsalted peanuts, toasted
5–6 teaspoons dry shrimp, ground

SALAD DRESSING
1/4 cup fish sauce
1/2 cup brown sugar
1/2 cup lime juice
2 garlic cloves, chopped

To make the dressing, combine all the ingredients and set aside.

Grate the papaya, then rinse in cold water and drain well. Toss the papaya with the salad dressing and add the bird's eye chillies, if liked. They will add spiciness to the salad. Add a teaspoon of peanuts and a teaspoon of ground shrimp and toss thoroughly.

Garnish the salad with the remaining peanuts and ground shrimp and serve immediately.

pictured right

San Francisco cioppino

serves 5   UNITED AIRLINES

2 small onions, chopped

1 1/2 tablespoons minced garlic

1/2 cup olive oil

1 teaspoon jalapeño pepper, deseeded and minced

2 small bay leaves

1/2 tablespoon chopped fresh thyme

125 g carrots, julienned

400 g canned tomatoes, diced

1/2 cup white wine

3 cups chicken stock

1/2 teaspoon saffron threads

1/2 cup tomato purée

250 g fresh mussels (meat only)

400 g fresh scallops, side muscle removed

350 g shrimp, tails removed, peeled and deveined

salt and freshly ground black pepper

2 teaspoons chopped fresh coriander

75 g cooked crab meat

To make the broth, sauté the onions and garlic in the olive oil in a large heavy-based saucepan for 3 minutes. Add the jalapeños, bay leaves, fresh thyme and carrots and continue to sauté for a further 3 minutes. Add the tomatoes, white wine, chicken stock, saffron and tomato purée and simmer for 20 minutes. Add the mussels, scallops and shrimp and bring to the boil. Remove from the heat, season to taste, and add the fresh coriander. Chill in a shallow pan to prevent the seafood from cooking any further. Gently fold in the crab meat just before serving.

pictured left

eggplant tarts with goat's cheese and basil-flavoured butter

serves 4   *Danio Braga* VARIG

2 medium eggplants

2 tablespoons coarse salt

2 tablespoons olive oil

4 shortcrust pastry tart shells

3 ripe tomatoes, sliced

fresh basil leaves

200 g goat's cheese, sliced

BASIL-FLAVOURED BUTTER

80 g unsalted butter

2 teaspoons fine salt

fresh basil leaves

Preheat the oven to 140°C.

To prepare the eggplants, cut crosswise into 1 cm thick slices, cover in coarse salt and place on an inclined tray to drain for 20 minutes. Wash to remove the salt, and pat dry. Spread one side of each slice with a little olive oil and grill under a medium heat until tender but firm.

To assemble the tarts, alternately layer a slice of eggplant, tomato, basil and goat's cheese into the tart shells, repeating three times, before finishing with a slice of tomato. Bake in the oven for 15 minutes.

Meanwhile, make the basil-flavoured butter. Place the butter, salt and basil leaves in a double boiler and heat gently until the butter has melted.

The tarts should be served hot. Place one tart in the centre of each plate, pour over the basil-flavoured butter and garnish with a fresh basil leaf.

pictured right

In CELEBRATING our 65th ANNIVERSARY, Ansett acknowledges its key business partners and the role they have played in ANSETT being recognised as one of the WORLD'S GREAT AIRLINES. The Gallery of Excellence features Ansett Australia's KEY BUSINESS PARTNERS. These are the core companies and organisations that work with Ansett Australia and who, through the EXCELLENCE of their products and services, contribute to the QUALITY of Ansett's own product and CUSTOMER SERVICES, both in-flight and on the ground.

Long Gully Estate Vineyard.

The Boeing Company

7755 E. Marginal Way S.
Seattle WA 98108 USA

PO Box 3707, M/C 10-06
Seattle WA
98124-2207 USA

Phone: 1 206 655 6123

Fax: 1 206 655 3987

Mr Phil Condit
*Chairman and Chief
Executive Officer*

Mr Harry Stonecipher
*President and Chief
Operating Officer*

Website:
www.boeing.com

The Boeing Company brings together the technology, products and know-how of two heritage companies – Rockwell and McDonnell Douglas. Its history is the most distinguished in world aviation. Boeing's relationship with Australia began more than 60 years ago with the export of commercial and military aircraft to Australia. Boeing helped establish Australia's aerospace industry in the 1930s and has been an integral part of its growth ever since, providing the technology, products and services that are the backbone of Australia's commercial and military aircraft fleets.

Boeing and Ansett have worked together as Ansett Australia has become one of the world's most respected airlines. In 1953 Ansett introduced the Douglas DC-6 to its fleet. In 1964 and 1967, Ansett took delivery of its first 727-100 and DC-9 aircraft, respectively. In 1973, the carrier modernised its fleet, replacing its 727-100 fleet with 727-200s.

Expanding its domestic route network, Ansett acquired its first Boeing 767-200 in 1983 and first 737-300 in 1986. In 1994, Ansett International's first 747 'Spaceships' began flying to Japan and Hong Kong. Currently, Ansett Australia and Ansett International operate 34 Boeing aircraft: 22 737-300s, 10 767-200/-300s and two 747-400s.

Boeing congratulates Ansett Australia on its 65th anniversary and is pleased to have been part of a shared history. We are grateful for the confidence you have placed in our products and value the relationship between our two companies. Boeing looks forward to continuing the partnership with Ansett Australia in the 21st century.

Boeing 747-300

Crown – A World of Entertainment

ACN: 006 973 262

CROWN

A WORLD OF ENTERTAINMENT.

8 Whiteman Street

Southbank VIC 3006

Phone: 61 3 9292 8888

Fax: 61 3 9292 6600

Email: walterw@crownltd.
com.au

Mr Walter Wagner
*Executive General Manager
Food & Beverage*

Website:
www.crownltd.com.au

Crown features five signature restaurants which offer an unprecedented selection of dining venues within a single hotel property. The dining options continue on the gaming floor with Mings, a spectacular traditional Cantonese restaurant. You can sample one of the casino's casual dining venues or dine in Australia's largest ballroom, the Palladium, Melbourne's most sought-after function venue, which can accommodate 2500 people and is the leading Australian and international entertainment venue.

Silks is Crown's prized signature restaurant. Silks combines the fine art of Cantonese cuisine presented in the elegant setting of a Chinese mansion.

Koko is a modern teppanyaki restaurant which includes à la carte dining with a sushi and sake bar. Koko also offers private teppanyaki and tatami rooms.

The all-day restaurant, Conservatory, serves breakfast, lunch and dinner, offering both buffet and à la carte options.

Breezes is adjacent to the hotel's spectacular spa and serves modern Australian cuisine with Mediterranean flavours.

JJ's Bar & Grill is a secluded and intimate dining venue that features steak and fresh seafood from the grill with premium champagnes from around the world.

Crown has established its position in the marketplace as offering a premier selection of dining experiences in Melbourne. Industry peers have recognised Crown's achievement for excellence in service and cuisine, making Crown one of Melbourne's premium dining precincts, offering choice, quality and memorable dining experiences to suit a diverse range of culinary palates.

gallery of excellence

Crown Towers - Above all Expectations

ACN: 006 973 262

8 Whiteman Street

Southbank VIC 3006

Phone: 61 3 9292 6666

Fax: 61 3 9292 6600

Email: hotelreservations
@crownltd.com.au

Mr Bryan Hiscock
*Executive General Manager
Crown Towers*

Website:
www.crownltd.com.au

Melbourne's Crown Towers is arguably Victoria's most luxurious hotel property and has become the benchmark of five-star hotels in Australia. Crown Towers specialises in catering to the business traveller and corporate guest. These guests are able to further enjoy the luxury, comfort and privacy of Crown Towers by reserving a Crystal Club room or suite. The Crystal Club is an exclusive lounge facility located on level 29. In this private world in the sky, guests enjoy 24-hour refreshments, complimentary breakfast to midday, and access to the extraordinary services of the Crystal Club lounge, Melbourne's premier Executive Floor.

The Crystal Club's library and lounge with their discreet location and spectacular views are the perfect setting for business and entertaining and a welcome retreat at the end of an arduous day.

All corporate guests have the option of Crystal Club access regardless of whether they are staying in a villa, suite or deluxe guestroom. Those corporate guests staying in a suite at the listed suite rate receive complimentary access to the Crystal Club.

Crown has 33 individually themed lavish villas, each with the character and ambience of a fine penthouse residence.

Crown Towers is firmly entrenched as Australia's premier hotel and offers corporate guests the most extensive range of facilities in the country. For your next visit to Melbourne, for business or pleasure, we invite you to come and experience Crown's unparalleled level of services and facilities.

Airspeed

Gate Gourmet International AG

ACN: 006 973 262

an SAirRelations Company

Gate Gourmet
International AG

Flughofstrasse 54

CH1852 Glattbrugg
Switzerland

PO Box QV

CH8058 Zurich Airport

Switzerland

Phone: 41 1 812 5480

Fax: 41 1 810 9175

Email: jwdankelman@
gategourmet.com

Mr Henning Boysen
President & CEO

Mr Odd Engebretsen
*President Division
Asia - Pacific*

Website:
www.gategourmet.com

Gate Gourmet, one of the world's leading airline catering companies, is part of the SAir Group – formerly the Swissair Group. We service over 200 airline customers worldwide with a global customer base that includes leading international carriers noted for the high standard of their inflight service and catering.

Gate Gourmet currently operates 150 kitchens in 6 continents and produces 798,000 meals per day or 291 million meals per year. Australia is a key market within our Division Asia-Pacific and promises to be one of significant future growth. Established here early in 1999, we now operate in seven cities Australia-wide.

Gate Gourmet is particularly proud to have been chosen as the base-catering supplier of Ansett Australia through the acquisition of Ansett inflight kitchens. Ansett Australia has a reputation for being a leader in style and innovation in their inflight catering, both on domestic and international routes. This reputation has resulted in international recognition and awards.

As a supplier of catering services, Gate Gourmet plays an important role in supporting the Ansett inflight product design and development. It is our challenge, through our partnership with Ansett, not only to provide consistent high-quality services but also to be attuned to the need for development and constant improvement.

We look forward to these challenges, confident that we will be able to use our global resources in order to establish a high international standard of operation in Australia.

Harrison Systems Integration Pty Ltd

ACN: 000 273 450

Sydney

10 Cahill Street

Camperdown NSW 2050

Phone: 61 2 9550 1700

Fax: 61 2 9565 2284

Melbourne

Phone: 61 3 9686 9090

Brisbane

Phone: 61 7 3847 2999

Adelaide

Phone: 61 8 8410 2727

Perth

Phone: 61 8 9421 1667

Email: info@harrisonsolutions.com

Website: www.harrisonsolutions.com

Mr Jim Harrison
Chairman

Mr Graeme Harrison
Director

Harrison Systems Integration (HSI) and Harrison Data Capture (HDC) provide the latest in information technology – including comprehensive Internet-based delivery applications – to corporate, business and government. HSI is also a significant developer of image and optical filing technology.

In the critical area of financial data, Ansett Financial Services has chosen HSI's WINoptic™ software to archive, index and retrieve accounting documents. WINoptic™ is an integrated archiving solution that allows immediate recall on any PC screen in an organisation of any prior records, whether the material was originally paper, computer reports, word processing or other files. It can be used as a total solution or can 'back-end' other supplier products.

HDC is at the forefront in IT outsourcing and provides business software and data processing solutions using internet technology. HDC also provides a specialist bureau service for data entry or combined scanning/indexing, with blind verification providing data entry in any format and images in any imaging system format. Services include: document scanning to CD; electronic archives; data warehousing; key punch and verify; web retrieval of images; microfilm and fiche conversion; client site services; forms/voucher processing; remittance processing; barcode recognition; OCR and mark recognition; and handwriting recognition.

To see how Harrison's products and services can assist your business, please visit our website. www.harrisonsolutions.com

IBM Australia Limited

ACN: 000 024 733

55 Coonara Avenue

West Pennant Hills
NSW 2125

Phone: 13 24 26

Website:
www.ibm.com.au

The partnership between Ansett and IBM began when Ansett was establishing itself as a national domestic airline and IBM was in the fledgling office products business. The real cornerstone of the relationship was laid in the 1960s when the Passenger Airline Reservation System (PARS) was deployed on IBM computer systems. This critical step provided real-time service to customers in a growing and increasingly competitive market.

In 1973 Ansett called on IBM to develop a computerised reservations system—ANSAMATIC—an acronym of Ansett and automatic. This was considered one of the most advanced in the world at the time. In 1976, Ansett was the first Australian airline to introduce computerised ticketing with the Ansarite system. This was followed in 1982 by Ansacare, an airline reservations system dedicated to the travel needs of disabled passengers.

Ansett and IBM have developed a number of mission-critical applications to improve the airline's customer service and operational efficiency. In the early 1990s, IBM worked with Ansett to implement the Merlin reservation system, the kernel for the highly successful e-Ticket and Global Rewards initiatives.

In recent years Ansett has entrusted IBM Global Services Australia with the management of its key information technology infrastructure and operations, allowing Ansett to concentrate on its core business.

IBM is committed to working with Ansett to address today's business needs and to position the company to meet future challenges. Our business relationship is based on mutual respect and trust that involves working together to exploit technology for business benefits.

*Left: David Thodey,
Managing Director
and CEO, IBM
Australia and
New Zealand.*

*Below: The IBM
Team for Ansett.
Left to right –
Gary Trytell,
Sach Sachdeva
and Richard Payne.*

*Left: Colleen Arnold,
Managing Director
and CEO, IBM Global
Services Australia.*

PRC-DeSoto Australia Pty Ltd

ACN: 050 106 217

PRC-DeSoto
International

23 Ovata Drive

Tullamarine VIC 3043

Phone: 61 3 9335 1557

Fax: 61 3 9335 3490

Email:
robert.barry@prc-desoto.com

Mr Robert Barry
Business Manager

Ms Anne Neeson
Assistant Business Manager

Website:
www.prc-desoto.com

We seal, bond, protect and decorate in more aerospace applications than anyone else in the world. We are PRC–DeSoto International – one global source for more than 1400 polymer-based products that are fundamental to aerospace manufacturing, maintenance and repair processes.

Ansett Australia, along with all leading airline companies, knows and uses our premier brands. These are PRC sealants, DeSoto and Celomer coatings, and Semco dispensing cartridges and application systems for multicomponent materials. Our brands have been recognised for quality, consistency, ease of use and convenience for over five decades.

Boeing 727-100

SalesForce Australia Pty Ltd

ACN: 006 688 955

33 Lincoln Square South

Carlton VIC 3053

Phone: 61 3 9287 9777

Fax: 61 3 9287 9774

Email:
mailus@salesforce.com.au

Mr Kevin Panozza
Managing Director

Mr Derrick Clayton
*Business Development
Manager*

Website:
www.salesforce.com.au

It's the recipe for a great customer relationship! After 65 years of outstanding service, Ansett knows a thing or two about building strong customer relationships. And for the past decade, they've relied on SalesForce to help them. As the largest call centre provider in Australia, SalesForce helps some of Australia's most dynamic companies build and manage their customer partnerships. Our clients include National Australia Bank, Medibank Private, Ericsson, Telstra and Fly Buys.

We're very proud of our association with Ansettt – they were our very first client. From an original team of 10 people, our Ansett team has grown to over 300. On behalf of Ansett we maintain regular contact with thousands of Ansett corporate clients and answer inbound calls from Ansett Golden Wing Club and Global Rewards members. Via advanced technology, our new Customer Contact Centres transparently manage telephone, fax, email, web chat and voice over Internet. Customer enquiries are immediately routed to the person who can help them, improving customer satisfaction, building loyalty and enhancing the brand relationship.

SalesForce. Bringing your customers closer.

gallery of excellence

Unisys Australia Limited

ARBN: 000 002 086

UNISYS

213 Miller Street
North Sydney NSW 2060
PO Box 448
Milsons Point NSW 1565
Phone: 61 2 9931 6666
Fax: 61 2 9957 3370

Mr Ron Frankenfield
*Vice President
and General Manager,
Unisys South Pacific*

Mr Peter Von Moltke
*Vice President
and General Manager,
Transportation,
Asia & South Pacific*

Website:
www.unisys.com.au

Unisys is an electronic business solutions company whose 35,000 employees help customers in 100 countries apply information technology to seize opportunities and meet the challenges of the new Internet economy.

Our customers worldwide include major airlines, major financial institutions, some of the world's best-known newspapers, and government and commercial organisations.

Unisys offers a rich portfolio of Unisys e-@ction Solutions for electronic business based on our expertise in 'repeatable' vertical industry solutions, network services, outsourcing, systems integration and multivendor support. We also supply enterprise-class servers and related technologies.

gallery of excellence

Boeing 737-200

The Allens Arthur Robinson Group

Allens Arthur Robinson

Allen Allen & Hemsley

2 Chifley Square

Sydney NSW 2000

Phone: 61 2 9230 4000

Fax: 61 2 9230 5333

Contact:
Mr Ian Wallace *Partner*
ian.wallace@allens.com.au

Group and associated offices

Sydney, Melbourne, Brisbane, Perth, Adelaide, Gold Coast, Port Moresby, Singapore, Hong Kong, Jakarta, Shanghai, Bangkok.

Arthur Robinson & Hedderwicks

Stock Exchange Centre

530 Collins Street

Melbourne VIC 3000

Phone: 61 3 9614 1011

Fax: 61 3 9614 4661

Contact:
Ms Wendy Peter *Partner*
wendy.peter@arh.com.au

The Allens Arthur Robinson Group
has enjoyed a long and close relationship with Ansett Australia. We are proud to be partners with Ansett Australia in its ongoing achievement of outstanding success in Australian and international aviation.

Allens Arthur Robinson is an alliance of leading Australian law firms — Allen Allen & Hemsley, Arthur Robinson & Hedderwicks and Finlaysons. We are recognised as having achieved outstanding success as Australian and international lawyers, thanks to key clients like Ansett Australia. We have 'on the ground' local knowledge, international expertise and an extensive and integrated network of offices across the Asia-Pacific region.

Ansett Air Freight

ACN: 000 495 269

 ANSETTAIRFREIGHT

A division of TNT Australia Pty Limited ACN 000 495 269

Level 6
Tower 2 TNT Plaza
Lawson Square

Redfern NSW 2016

PO Box 1803

Strawberry Hills
NSW 2012

Phone: 61 2 9319 8000

Fax: 61 2 9319 8020

Mr Wally Bell
General Manager

Mr David Howlett
*National Sales
& Marketing Manager*

Website: www.aaf.com.au

Since 1980 our people at Ansett Air Freight have delivered freight across Australia. Ansett Air Freight was a wholly owned division of Ansett Australia until the business was purchased by TNT Australia Pty Ltd in June 1999. Ansett Air Freight's association with Ansett Australia continues through Ansett Australia providing air linehaul which enables Ansett Air Freight to deliver freight in the most timely and efficient manner.

Ansett Air Freight has five express service levels: Priority One (same day), Overnight First Class, Economy, Standby and Prepaid. Consignment tracking is available via the Internet at our website www.aaf.com.au.

Avis Australia

Level 2
15 Bourke Street

Mascot NSW 2020

Phone: 61 2 9353 9033

Fax: 61 2 9353 9090

Mr George Proos
*Vice President &
Managing Director*

Mr Greg Petersen
*Sales & Marketing
Director*

Website:
www.avis.com/
local_hp/australia

Avis is proud to help celebrate Ansett Australia's 65th anniversary. Ansett's 65-year tradition of excellence in serving Australian travellers mirrors Avis' commitment to those travellers when they reach their destination.

Our commitment to high quality customer services has led to more customer service awards than any other car rental company. We have also initiated unique customer services such as Avis Preferred, Avis Rapid Return and most recently Avis Navigator.

When Ansett introduced their Frequent Flyer program, they selected Avis to become an exclusive partner, because at Avis, we try harder.

Avis is the official Provider of Rental Cars to the Sydney 2000 Olympic Games.

Bain International

ACN: 003 850 619

BAIN INTERNATIONAL

Level 35
The Chifley Tower

2 Chifley Square

Sydney NSW 2000

Phone: 61 2 9229 1600

Fax: 61 2 9223 2404

Email:
adam.warden@bain.com

Mr Adam Warden
Partner

Mr Paul Meehan
Partner

Website: www.bain.com

As a relatively new partner in Ansett Australia's 65 years of history, Bain International is proud to be associated with Ansett's Business Recovery Program. In partnership with Ansett's management and staff, we have supported the ongoing effort to improve the service and product offerings to valued business and leisure travellers, whilst ensuring sustainable long-term profitability. We wish Ansett's staff and management continued success in the pursuit of their 'Great Airline – Great Business' vision.

Boeing 767-200

Clemenger Direct

ACN: 006 126 549

CLEMENGER DIRECT

4/553 St Kilda Road

Melbourne VIC 3004

Phone: 61 3 9526 2200

Fax: 61 3 9526 2202

Email: clemenger.
direct@clemenger.com.au

Ms Jane Tubb
Group Managing Director

Mr Andrew Hockley
Executive Director

Website:
www.clemenger
direct.com.au

Clemenger Direct is Australia's leading agency in direct marketing, with a commitment to delivering breakthrough strategies and visionary creative solutions. With offices in Melbourne, Sydney and Brisbane, Clemenger Direct has enormous resources as well as the ability to integrate sophisticated database and digital marketing solutions into any client's communications program.

Concorde International Travel Ltd

ACN: 003 237 189

403 George Street

Sydney NSW 2000

Phone: 61 2 9244 2222

Fax: 61 2 9290 3641

Mr Leslie Cassar
Group Managing Director

Mr Eddy Baldacchino
Chairman

Website:
www.concorde.com.au

Concorde International Travel, Australia's most innovative travel company, is the largest supplier of airline tickets to Australian travel agents. The company's representation arm, World Aviation Systems, is the largest airline representation operation in the world, providing sales and marketing management to some 50 airlines. Concorde's package holiday division produces leading brand holidays to the USA, New Zealand and Indochina from Australia, and to Australia and New Zealand from our North American offices. Concorde also provides dynamic e-commerce and processing technology to Australian, New Zealand and South African travel companies.

From one industry pioneer to another, Concorde International Travel congratulates Ansett Australia on its 65th anniversary.

DMR Consulting Group (Australia) Pty Ltd

ACN: 006 091 774

Level 8
1 Southbank Boulevard

Southbank VIC 3006

Phone: 61 3 9924 3000

Fax: 61 3 9924 3001

Email: dmr.asia.pacific
@apac.dmr.com.au

Mr Alan Baxter
President

Dr John Adams
General manager

Website: www.dmr.com

DMR is proud to have been a supporter of Ansett Australia, providing it with business and information technology (IT) services since 1992.

DMR Consulting Group is a leading international provider of management consulting and IT services to businesses and public enterprises, with more than 60 offices in Australia, the Asia-Pacific region, the United States, Canada and Europe. With 1998 revenues exceeding $US850 million and a global base of close to 10,000 professionals worldwide, DMR is known for providing integrated business and IT solutions that enable clients to improve their competitive position, market share and productivity.

Foodservice Equipment International Pty Limited

ACN: 003 429 605

51 Chard Road

Brookvale NSW 2100

Phone: 61 2 9938 5000

Fax: 61 2 9938 5055

Email:
tableware@fei.com.au

Mr John Leith
Chief Executive Officer

Ms Gail Leith
Managing Director

When Ansett Australia decided to introduce superior Business/First Class, FEI, together with the Rosenthal Group and WMF of Germany, were delighted to participate as design and supply partners from Day One.

Our challenge? To create perfect chinaware from Rosenthal, perfect cutlery and servingware from WMF complementing Ansett's perfect inflight service. Together we achieved Ansett's expectations. A combination of simple design and perfect functionality, and, naturally we kept our promise to deliver on time and within budget.

FEI, Rosenthal and WMF are extremely proud of our role in helping Ansett Australia become the airline awarded the 'best business class in the world'!

Bristol 170 MK21

George Patterson Bates Advertising

ACN: 004 198 341

 **GEORGE PATTERSON** BATES

Level 2
162 Collins Street

Melbourne VIC 3000

GPO Box 1757Q

Melbourne VIC 3001

Phone: 61 3 9287 1200

Fax: 61 3 9287 1400

Mr Ian Elliott
Chief Executive Officer

Mr Hamish McLennan
Managing Director

To maintain a level of excellence in any industry is difficult. To do so in the competitive airline industry is an achievement in itself.

For 65 years, Ansett Australia has unwaveringly demonstrated its obsession with being the best. From innovations on the ground, to those 'little touches' in flight, millions upon millions of passengers have grown to expect something different from Ansett. And is it any surprise that some of the biggest names in the airline industry today are beginning to ask the question, *how do they do it?*

Here's to 65 years of doing it right.

Hotel Enterprize

ACN: 057 989 376

44 Spencer Street

Melbourne VIC 3000

Phone: 61 3 9629 6991

Fax: 61 3 9614 7963

Email:
entrpriz@ozemail.com.au

Ms Barbara Ralph
Chairman

Mr Hedley Elliot
Managing Director

In a short four-year association with Ansett Australia, Hotel Enterprize has become a leader in package holidays and a major independent hotel dealing exclusively with the airline.

Location: Situated next to the Crown Casino Exhibition and Convention Centre, Hotel Enterprize is a newly refurbished three star hotel in Melbourne's CBD with the train and bus station 50 metres away. Work will be completed late 2000 on extensions that will double the size of the hotel enabling it to provide both three- and four-star rooms.

Rooms: Private facilities, air-conditioning/heating, mini bar, colour television, free in-house movies, tea/coffee facilities, refrigerator, radio alarm clock, ISD/IDD direct dial phones.

LINK Recruitment Group

ACN: 071 334 257

Level 16
600 Bourke Street

Melbourne VIC 3000

Phone: 61 3 9608 6222

Fax: 61 3 9670 3402

Email: link@linkrg.com

Mr Chris Malin
Managing Director

Mr Steve Roberts
Director

Website:
www.linkrg.com

LINK Recruitment Group is built on a foundation of specialist recruitment services. Our primary business is recruiting accounting, finance, information technology (IT), legal and administrative support staff for industry, commerce, education and government sectors. Our processes are quality accredited to ISO 9002 series level and we meet all Recruitment and Consulting Services Association (RCSA) standards.

We see our specialisation as our strength. Specialist services include Accountancy LINK, LINK Technology, LINK Finance, LINK Legal, LINK Secretarial; and our national network of offices and international affiliate network give our clients access to a wide range of resources.

We pride ourselves on providing a quality service that surpasses the high expectations of our clients.

Maddock Lonie & Chisholm Lawyers

Maddock Lonie & Chisholm
LAWYERS

140 Williams Street

Melbourne VIC 3000

Phone: 61 3 9288 0555

Fax: 61 3 9288 0666

Email:
info@maddocks.com.au

Mr David Laidlaw
Chairman of Partners

Mr Guy O'Connor
Managing Partner

Website:
www.maddocks .com.au

At Maddock Lonie & Chisholm we place great value on our relationship with Ansett and our work as their legal advisers on major projects, including the domestic passenger terminal at Sydney Airport. We commend Ansett's achievements over the past 65 years.

As a leading commercial law firm, our clients include top organisations from the private and public sectors, both in Australia and overseas.

Our affiliation with ADVOC Asia and ADVOC Europe positions us strongly for working across international boundaries to better serve our clients in this increasingly global environment.

ADVOC is an association of independent commercial law firms providing access to local networks and appropriate legal advice in Asia and the Pacific Rim, and Europe.

Convair CV340

Memorex Telex Asia-Pacific

ACN: 000 835 487

3 Thomas Holt Drive

North Ryde NSW 2113

Phone: 61 2 9805 5805

Fax: 61 2 9805 0420

Email: marketing
@mtxaspac.com.au

Mr Bruce Stewart
Managing Director

Mr Philip Pickering
Services Director

Website:
mtxaspac.com.au

Memorex Telex, one of Australia's leading network integrators, has a 30-year history in enterprise computing. We specialise in delivering solutions and services for business-critical networks. Memorex Telex is service focused, delivering a complete range of solutions from maintenance services through to total network solutions.

Ansett Australia and Memorex Telex have mutually benefited from a strong business relationship for the past 23 years, from the comprehensive maintenance of Ansett's business-critical equipment around the world, to desktop support in partnership with IBM Global Services Australia. We look forward to a continued successful relationship with Ansett and congratulate the company on its first 65 years.

Morgan & Banks Limited

ACN: 002 884 424

Morgan & Banks

Level 11
Grosvenor Place

225 George Street

Sydney NSW 2000

Locked Bag 19
Grosvenor Place

Sydney NSW 2000

Phone: 61 2 9256 0333

Fax: 61 2 9251 3975

Email: info@morganbanks.
com.au

Mr Geoff Morgan
Chairman
TMP Australasia

Mr Alistair Sutherland
Australasian
Managing Director

Website:
www.morganbanks.
com.au

Morgan & Banks congratulates Ansett Australia on its 65th anniversary. As one of the world's leading international human resources organisations, Morgan & Banks is proud to be in partnership with one of the world's leading airlines. With more than 6100 employees in 25 countries, Morgan & Banks has joined TMP Worldwide to form the world's leading provider of global human resources solutions, incorporating traditional and online recuitment, together with human resources consulting activities.

Nortel Networks

How the world shares ideas.

ACN: 003 164 145

593–595 Blackburn Road
Notting Hill VIC 3168
Phone: 61 3 9263 6600
Fax: 61 3 9263 6666

Mr Chris Sarsfield
*Business Development
Manager
Enterprise Solutions*

Mr Paul Murphy
*State Sales Manager
Victoria
Enterprise Solutions*

Nortel Networks and Ansett Australia recognise each other's best-of-breed qualities. Nortel Networks is the preferred supplier of Ansett's telecommunications systems and call centre services. Ansett is Nortel Networks' carrier of choice.

Nortel Networks offers customers many business advantages by bringing telephony, video and data together in a single unified network. This Unified Networks vision enables customers to deliver multimedia applications and reap the benefits of electronic commerce driven by the Internet.

With extensive product portfolio and depth of experience in telephony and data networks, Nortel Networks is the first vendor to offer service providers and enterprises across-the-board expertise in every major communications technology.

PAC Australia Pty Ltd

ACN: 067 506 236

AS/NZS ISO 9001 : 1994
Reg No 322
PO Box 409
Canterbury VIC 3126
Phone: 61 3 9543 5548
Fax: 61 3 9543 5508
Email:
pacaust@enternet.com.au

Ms Janet Fenech
Managing Director

Mr Ron Fenech
Director

Website:
www.pacaustralia.com.au

PAC Australia is proud to acknowledge its association as a key partner with Ansett Australia for the past decade, specialising in aircraft cabin soft furnishings and decor.

PAC Australia's integrity in maintaining competitiveness and quality is vital. This is achieved by a highly successful quality assurance system accredited to AS/NZS ISO 9001 that incorporates necessary industry regulations and a company-wide commitment that sees customer satisfaction as an integral part of the organisation.

PAC Australia offers consulting services complete through to the finished appearance, catering for all types of cabin interiors from regional to international aircraft, transport, hospitality, entertainment and associated industries.

Douglas DC-3

Salmat Pty Ltd

ACN: 067 506 236

152 Miller Road
Chester Hill NSW 2162

Phone: 61 2 9724 0155

Fax: 61 2 9726 9895

Email:
marketing@salmat.com.au

Mr Peter Mattick
Joint Managing Director

Mr Phil Salter
Joint Managing Director

Website:
www.salmat.com.au

Salmat, Australia's leading direct customer communications organisation, is proud of its six-year partnership with Ansett Australia.

Salmat is dedicated to the highest standard of customer service. We pride ourselves on delivering the best in customer communications through voice, paper and online. Through our partnership, Ansett customers receive important information about the Golden Wing Club program. Whether it's about new reward offerings, its participation in the Star Alliance group, confirming electronic ticket purchases or ensuring members know the number of points accumulated through monthly statements, Salmat is part of this communication. We congratulate Ansett Australia on 65 years of success.

Seven Network Limited

ACN: 052 816 789

Level 13
1 Pacific Highway

North Sydney NSW 2060

Phone: 61 2 9967 7777

Fax: 61 2 9967 7773

Mr Kerry Stokes
Executive Chairman

Ms Maureen Plavsic
*Director, Sales and
Corporate Marketing*

Website:
www.seven.com.au

As the Australian television landscape moves from the traditional five free-to-air television networks to dozens of channels, unique brand positioning will become more important for consumers to navigate a world of excess choice. Distinctive, high-quality programming, innovative technology and a unique connection with the community will distinguish the Seven brand.

A key element of the Seven brand is its leadership in bringing major events to all Australians. Major projects for Seven underpin this approach: the Sydney Olympic Games, its principal sponsorhip of Opera Australia and its involvement in significant projects such as the development of the Colonial Stadium and Broadcast Centre in Melbourne.

AAV Business Communications

AAV Business Communications is proud to produce Ansett Australia's video and audio inflight entertainment as well as a range of specialty videos and branding packages. AAV Business Communications' services also include creative development, strategic advice, video production, interactive communications (CD-ROM, websites, e-commerce), business theatre, events, exhibitions and business television.

180 Bank Street

South Melbourne VIC 3205

PO Box 296

South Melbourne VIC 3205

Phone: 61 3 9251 1700

Fax: 61 3 9690 8841

Mr Tim McMahon
General Manager

Mr Andris Pinnis
Manager

Website:
www.aavbc.com.au
Email:
tmcmahon@aavbc.com.au

Accor

ACN: 009 175 820

Accor is Australia's – and the world's – largest hotel operator, with renowned hotel brands such as Sofitel, Novotel, Mercure and Ibis. Accor's hotel network includes both central city locations and prime resort areas. Voted 'Hotel Group of the Year' twice in the past three years in the National Tourism Industry Awards, Accor is a major partner of Ansett Australia.

Level 46, MLC Centre
19-29 Martin Place

Sydney NSW 2000

Phone: 61 2 9367 0888

Fax: 61 2 9367 0899

Mr David Baffsky
Chairman

Mr Michael Issenberg
Managing Director

Website:
www.hotelweb.fr

Airbus Industrie

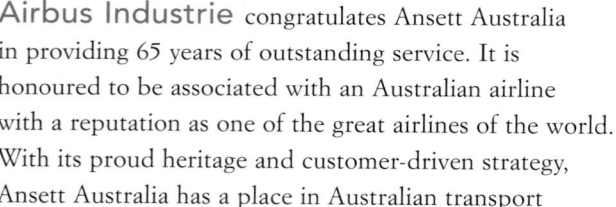

Airbus Industrie congratulates Ansett Australia in providing 65 years of outstanding service. It is honoured to be associated with an Australian airline with a reputation as one of the great airlines of the world. With its proud heritage and customer-driven strategy, Ansett Australia has a place in Australian transport history as enduring as that of Cobb & Co.

Ansett Australia was one of the first airlines outside Europe to operate Airbus Industrie's A320 Skystar. Airbus Industrie is a leading manufacturer of commercial airliners seating between 100 and 450 passengers. It sets the standard, winning half of all sales and offering airlines and passengers the most modern aircraft family in the world.

Website: www.airbus.com

Air Canada

Canada's flagship air carrier is recognised as a leader in the global air transportation market by pursuing a strategy based on value-added customer service, technical excellence and passenger safety. Air Canada's extensive global network, schedules and customer services are enhanced through the Star Alliance network.

Air Canada Centre

PO Box 14,000
Station Airport

Dorval Quebec

Canada H4Y 1H4

Phone: 1 514 422 5000

Mr John Fraser
Chairman of Air Canada

Mr Robert Milton
*President & CEO
of Air Canada*

Website:
www.aircanada.ca

Airbus A320-200

Ansett Australia Chauffeur Drive

ACN: 010 237 108

ANSETT AUSTRALIA
CHAUFFEUR DRIVE

Chauffeur Drive offers an extensive range of chauffeur driven vehicles, from executive sedans through to large luxury coaches. All of which can be utilised for airport transfers, sightseeing tours, personalised itineraries, large groups and conferences. Chauffeur Drive offer services in all our Australian capital cities and can be utilised 24 hours a day.

Central Reservations

Phone: 61 2 9693 5827

Fax: 61 2 9693 5963

Mr Warren Healey
Managing Director

Mr John Demetre
*Director and Group
General Manager*

Australian Cricket Board

ACN: 006 089 130

The Australian Cricket Board prides itself on a history of long-standing, successful partnerships. Ansett Australia is an important part of our history, having been the official carrier of the Australian cricket team for 19 years and the major sponsor of Australian Test series since 1996/97. Congratulations on turning 65, Ansett.

90 Jolimont Street

Jolimont VIC 3002

Phone: 61 3 9653 9999

Fax: 61 3 9653 9911

Mr Denis W. Rogers
Chairman

Mr Malcolm W. Speed
Chief Executive Officer

Website:
www.baggygreen.com.au

Australian Football League

ACN: 004 155 211

The Australian Football League has enjoyed a partnership with Ansett Australia since 1989, when Ansett was appointed the AFL's official carrier. We were delighted when Ansett furthered their involvement in AFL football in 1995 by sponsoring the Ansett Australia Cup. The AFL congratulates Ansett Australia on its 65th anniversary.

MCG
Brunton Avenue

Jolimont VIC 3002

GPO Box 1449N

Melbourne VIC 3001

Phone: 61 3 9643 1999

Fax: 61 3 9654 4646

Mr Wayne Jackson
Chief Executive Officer

Mr Ron Evans
*Chairman AFL
Commission*

Website:
www.afl.com.au

Berri Limited

ACN: 008 077 889

Australian-owned Berri Limited is Australia's largest fruit juice manufacturer with annual sales of approximately $600 million. Berri, the leading imported juice brand in more than 20 overseas countries particularly throughout Asia and the Middle East, is committed to becoming a world-class processor and congratulates Ansett Australia on its 65th anniversary.

60 Jolimont Street

East Melbourne VIC 3002

PO Box 1000

East Melbourne VIC 3002

Phone: 61 3 9654 7577

Fax: 61 3 9658 8144

Mr John Cook
Managing Director

Mr Geoff Sawyer
Director of Sales

Website:
www.berriltd.com.au
Email:
kcamp@berriltd.com.au

gallery of excellence

Bliss-Fox Ground Support Equipment Pty Limited

ACN: 086 067 594

A subsidiary of Nepean Engineering,
we have supplied aircraft pushback and towing tractor requirements for Ansett Australia at Melbourne and Sydney International Terminals. Our GSE product range includes tractors and towbars for use with aircraft of all sizes. Our international success can be attributed to our ability to customise products to our customers' requirements.

6 Maxwell Place

Narellan NSW 2567

Phone: 61 2 4647 7979

Fax: 61 2 4647 7977

Email: admin@bliss-fox
-gse.com.au

Mr David Fuller
Managing Director

Mr Neil McPherson
General Manager

Website:
www.bliss-fox-gse.com.au

Boyer Group Pty Ltd

ACN: 007 305 179

Boyer Group has exclusive advertising signage rights at Australia's premier sporting venues including the Melbourne Cricket Ground, the Colonial Stadium and Stadium Australia – venues where the nation's biggest sporting events are played. Boyer Group is proud to have delivered Ansett Australia major brand exposure in sport for many years and congratulates them on their 65th anniversary.

1B Riddell Parade

Elsternwick VIC 3185

Phone: 61 3 9523 0644

Fax: 61 3 9523 0744

22/1 Market Street

Sydney NSW 2000

Phone: 61 2 9261 2255

Fax: 61 2 9267 9988

Caltex Australia Limited

ACN: 000 032 128

Caltex Australia Limited has been supplying fuel to Ansett Australia's fleet for more than 10 years. With refineries in Sydney and Brisbane, Caltex supplies more than 1.5 billion litres of jet fuel per year to Sydney, Brisbane, Melbourne and Cairns airports and is the largest supplier of jet fuel on Australia's eastern seaboard.

MLC Centre
19–29 Martin Place

Sydney NSW 2000

GPO Box 3916

Sydney NSW 2001

Phone: 61 2 9250 5000

Fax: 61 2 9250 5742

Mr Malcolm Irving
Chairman of Directors

Mr Ian Blackburne
Managing Director & CEO

Website:
www.caltex.com.au
Email:
rtarnaws@caltex.com.au

Com Tech Communications Pty Ltd

ACN: 003 371 239

Com Tech Communications, Australia's leading end-to-end network integrator, provides technical expertise, customer service and product support. Com Tech provides the complete range of networking services from network infrastructure design and implementation to Internet development and call centre applications. Com Tech and Ansett Australia have enjoyed a productive partnership since 1996.

Unit 5
37–41 Doody Street

Alexandria NSW 2015

PO Box 207

Alexandria NSW 2015

Phone: 61 2 9693 3088

Fax: 61 2 9669 5713

Mr David Shein
CEO & Managing Director

Mr Jon Shein
Director

Website:
www.comtech.com.au
Email:
sales@comtech.com.au

gallery of excellence

Douglas DC-6B

Connat Flight Services Pty Ltd

ACN: 064 142 418

Connat Flight Services began its association with Ansett Australia in Tasmania in 1981 and through Ansett's confidence, expanded to the mainland in 1991. Alpha Airports Group UK became our parent company in 1994. Connat now services airlines in Hobart, Launceston, Canberra, Townsville and the Gold Coast with the unmistakable Connat style.

2nd Floor
16 Queensland Avenue

Broadbeach QLD 4218

PO Box 1567

Broadbeach QLD 4218

Phone: 61 7 5592 5545

Fax: 61 7 5592 6632

Ms Yvonne Smith
Managing Director

Mr Peter Smith
Director

De Bortoli Wines Pty Limited

ACN: 000 146 672

De Bortoli (established 1928) has been a proud supplier to Ansett since 1994. It began with one wine, the acclaimed Noble One, and other wines have been represented over the years. We congratulate Ansett on its 65th anniversary and look forward to the continuing association between De Bortoli and Ansett.

PO Box 21

Bilbul NSW 2680

Phone: 61 2 6964 9444

Fax: 61 2 6964 9400

Mr Deen De Bortoli
Chairman

Mr Darren De Bortoli
Managing Director

Dowd Corporation Pty Ltd

ACN: 005 744 561

Dowd Corporation is proud to provide total outsource management of the corporate apparel requirements of Ansett. Servicing over 180,000 staff members in such organisations as Australia Post, ANZ, Air New Zealand, AMP and NAB amongst others, Dowd provides a service that is tailored to the needs of each client.

8–10 Hall Street

Hawthorn East VIC 3123

Locked Bag 18

Hawthorn PO VIC 3122

Phone: 61 3 9282 9666

Fax: 61 3 9822 8550

Email:
chrisw@dowdcorp.com.au

Mr John Laidlaw
Chairman

Mr Christopher Walter
Managing Director

Feltex Carpets Limited

Feltex Carpets Limited has been manufacturing carpet for the demanding commercial, hospitality, and transport markets for over 50 years and is proud of its long association with Ansett Australia. Feltex aircraft carpets meet the Boeing Material Standards and ISO 9001. All carpets are designed and manufactured to meet the unique requirements of individual airlines.

145 Symonds Street

Auckland New Zealand

PO Box 2884

Auckland New Zealand

Phone: 64 9 379 1910

Fax: 64 9 379 1912

Email: export@feltex.co.nz

Mr Chris Davis
Chief Executive Officer

Mr Luke Bunt
Chief Operating Officer

Website:
www.feltex.com

Group 4 Securitas Pty Limited

ACN: 001 375 186

Group 4 Securitas Pty Limited is the country's largest Australian-owned security organisation employing around 3000 security guards nationally. Group 4 Securitas provides passenger screening services for Ansett at all Australian domestic and international airports where required. We are proud to partner Ansett in providing the very highest standards of security and passenger screening.

495 Victoria Street

Gladesville NSW 2111

PO Box 141

Top Ryde NSW 2111

Phone: 61 2 9844 2000

Fax: 61 2 9844 2277

Mr John Schaeffer
Executive Chairman

Mr John Eriani
Executive Director

Website:
www.group4.com.au

Hamilton Island Enterprises Pty Ltd

ACN: 009 946 909

Hamilton Island is Australia's favourite Great Barrier Reef holiday destination. The island has a choice of four hotels, ten restaurants and an endless array of things to do. Hamilton Island has the only jet airport in the Whitsunday Islands, and has enjoyed a long relationship with Ansett Australia in making many special holiday memories.

Hamilton Island
Executive Office

Front Street

Hamilton Island
QLD 4803

Phone: 61 7 4946 9999

Fax: 61 7 4946 8888

Mr Wayne Kirkpatrick
*Chief Executive Officer
and Managing Director*

Mr Barry Atkins
*Director of Sales
and Marketing*

Reservations Freecall:
1800 075 110

Hawker de Havilland Components Pty Limited

ACN: 001 800 095

A wholly owned subsidiary of Tenix Pty Ltd, HdH Components is proud of its 50-year partnership with Ansett Australia. Formerly as Dunlop Aviation Division and BTR Aerospace Australia, the company provided technical support and supply of Dunlop UK manufactured wheels and brakes for Ansett aircraft including the Viscount, Fokker F27 and currently the British Aerospace BAe146.

836 Mountain Highway

Bayswater VIC 3153

Locked Bag 39

Bayswater VIC 3153

Phone: 61 3 9720 6166

Fax: 61 3 9720 4996

Mr D Glenk
General Manager

Mr R Young
*Sales and Marketing
Manager*

Email:
hdhcomp@hdh.com.au

Hayman

ACN: 070 662 627

Hayman, the jewel of the Great Barrier Reef, was named in the Top 3 Resorts and Hotels in the World in the internationally renowned Conde Nast Traveler's Readers Choice Awards for 1999. Hayman was also named Best Resort Pacific Rim. Hayman has consistently been the recipient of high-profile world awards.

Hayman

Great Barrier Reef

North Queensland 4801

Phone: 61 7 4940 1234

Fax: 61 7 4940 1567

Email:
reserve@hayman.com.au

Mr Jolyon Bulley
General Manager

Mr Heiner Werdeling
Resort Manager

Website:
www.hayman.com.au

BAe 146-200

Hewlett-Packard Australia Limited

ACN: 004 394 763

Hewlett-Packard is proud to support Ansett Australia in celebrating its 65th anniversary. As the steward of open systems, HP's e-services help people and businesses derive new value from the Internet by moving beyond web-based access to information, to a world where people simply plug-in to a rich array of nimble, modular electronic services.

31-41 Joseph Street	Mr Bruce Thompson *Managing Director*
Blackburn North VIC 3230	
Phone: 13 13 47	Mr Alvin Colvin *Human Resources* *Director*
Fax: 61 3 9898 7831	

Website: www.hp.com

Hilton Hotels

ACN: 008 419 485

Hilton is delighted to be a preferred partner with Ansett Airlines and wishes Ansett every success on its 65th anniversary. Hilton also celebrates a milestone, 25 years of operation in Australia, with hotels in Adelaide, Brisbane, Cairns, Melbourne, Perth, Sydney and Sydney Airport and the opening of Hilton Melbourne Airport and Hilton Auckland in 2000.

259 Pitt Street	Mr Oded Lifschitz *Vice President* *Australasia*
Sydney NSW 2000	
GPO Box 3934	Mr Robin Wattera *Area Director* *Sales and Marketing* *Australasia*
Sydney NSW 2001	
Phone: 61 2 9266 2000	
Fax: 61 2 9265 6065	
Email: sales_sydney@hilton.com	Website: www.hilton.com

Hotel Lindrum

ACN: 068 035 683

HOTEL
LINDRUM

Hotel Lindrum, Melbourne's newest design hotel, provides corporate travellers with the ultimate in comfort. The boutique hotel has 59 spacious rooms and suites with modern appointments including CD/stereo systems, modem points and fax machines. With personal service, the emphasis is to create that relaxing 'club-like' atmosphere, a home away from home.

26 Flinders Street	Mr David Marringer *Managing Director*
Melbourne VIC 3000	
Phone: 61 3 9668 1111	Ms Kate Sears *General Manager*
Fax: 61 3 9668 1199	
Email: ksears@ hotellindrum.com.au	Website: www.hotellindrum.com.au

Hyatt Hotels & Resorts

ARBN: 003 184 076

HYATT
HOTELS & RESORTS

At Hyatt we believe a great hotel should offer more than a good night's sleep. It should offer an environment that awakens your senses. Subtle details giving each hotel and resort a personality as unique as its location. We are proud to be associated with Ansett Australia on its 65th anniversary.

7/504 Pacific Highway	Mr Willi Martin *Regional Director* *Pacific*
St Leonards NSW 2065	
Phone: 61 2 9433 3888	Ms Sheriden Walshe *Director of Marketing* *Pacific*
Fax: 61 2 9433 3826	
Email: vcamenzuli@hyatt.com.au	
	Website: www.hyatt.com.au

gallery of excellence

Long Gully Estate

Long Gully's 40-ha vineyard produces premium table wines, which have won countless trophies and medals around the world. Long Gully Estate and Ansett Australia have been associated for many years now, so, if you haven't tried these exquisite wines, they are available to Ansett customers in-flight across Australia.

PO Box 1073	R & I Klapp *Directors*
Windsor VIC 3181	
Phone: 61 3 9510 5798	O Klapp *General Manager*
Fax: 61 3 9510 9859	

Long Prosper Enterprise Co. Ltd

LPEC

Long Prosper is the largest supplier of in-flight entertainment headsets to airlines worldwide. A complete range of pneumatic and electronic headsets is offered as well as a new series of noise cancellation electronic headsets. Long Prosper offers these other products: scale model aircraft and duty free toy items.

10F, No 1093 Yu-Cheng Road	Mr David Huang *General Manager*
Ku-Shan District	
Kaohsiung Taiwan 804	Mr Jimmy Wu *Director of Engineering*
Phone: 886 7 5530723-7	
Fax: 886 7 5530731-2	
Email: Lpros@ms6.hinet.net	Website: www.Longprosper.com

Lyncroft Consulting Group

ACN: 050 199 249

Lyncroft Consulting Group is proud to partner Ansett Australia in building the airline's executive and management team. Lyncroft is committed to providing executive recruitment and human resource excellence across a range of specialist areas, including: Sales & Marketing, Engineering & Operations, Finance & Business Services, Technology & Telecommunications and Healthcare & Education.

Level 11 380 St Kilda Road	Mr Geoff Slade *Managing Director*
Melbourne VIC 3004	Mr Wayne Bruce *Chief Operating Officer*
Phone: 61 3 9235 5100	
Fax: 61 3 9235 5102	
Email: melbourne@lyncroft.com.au	Website: www.lyncroft.com.au

Mission Personnel Services Pty Ltd

ACN: 071 997 950

Mission Personnel Services, listed as one of the top 15 recruitment agencies in Australia, is proud to be associated with Ansett Australia. In an industry where technology changes daily, one thing remains constant – the need for committed people. Mission Personnel provides quality human resource solutions to meet all strategic needs.

Level 7, 490 Bourke Street	Mr Philip Desmet *Managing Director*
Melbourne VIC 3000	Ms Donna Desmet *Director*
GPO Box 4905VV	
Melbourne VIC 3001	
Phone: 61 3 9642 2221	Website: www.mission personnel.com.au
Fax: 61 3 9670 9996	Email: manager@ missionpersonnel.com.au

Vickers Vicount 700

National Rugby League

ACN: 082 088 962

The NRL is pleased to congratulate Ansett on its 65th anniversary. Through good times and bad, Ansett has been a loyal partner and demonstrated commitment, teamwork and loyalty. Week in and week out, the NRL relies on Ansett to transport its teams and referees. The game is strong because of partners such as Ansett.

Level 2
Art House Building

Bent Street

Fox Studios

Moore Park NSW 2001

Phone: 61 2 9339 8500

Fax: 61 2 9339 8505

Email: reception@nrl.com.au

Mr Malcolm Noad
Chairman

Mr David Moffett
Chief Executive Officer

Website:
www.nrl.com.au

Nutters Foods Pty Ltd

ACN: 004 375 875

Nutters Foods Pty Ltd are processors, packers and distributors of high-quality savoury snacks and dried fruits. For over 15 years Nutters has been a major supplier of packaged nuts and snacks to Ansett Australia, which provides complimentary packs to over 5 million passengers each year for its inflight catering services.

4 Mosrael Place

Rowville VIC 3178

PO Box 9034

Scoresby VIC 3179

Phone: 61 3 9764 9911

Fax: 61 3 9764 9477

Email: nuttersfoods@
bigpond.com.au

Mr Ron Sicree
Managing Director

QBE Insurance (Australia) Limited

ACN: 003 191 035

QBE Insurance has serviced the workers' compensation needs of Ansett Australia for over 15 years. Throughout this period we have developed an excellent partnership which has enabled us to meet the changing needs of this dynamic progressive airline. We congratulate Ansett Australia on its 65th anniversary.

82 Pitt Street

Sydney NSW 2000

Phone: 61 2 9375 4444

Fax: 61 2 9375 4316

Mr Frank O'Hallorhan
Managing Director

Mr Raymond Jones
General Manager

Website:
www.QBE.com.au

Senteq Information Systems

ACN: 003 035 756

Senteq Information Systems provides Ansett Australia with information technology and services to enable them to participate in the networked economy. Senteq is proud to partner Ansett, utilising its experience in network computing and e-business technology to generate increased profits and business opportunities. To find out more about us, visit www.senteq.com.au

11 Albany Street

St Leonards NSW 2065

Phone: 61 2 9391 0555

Fax: 61 2 9391 0566

Email:
sales@senteq.com.au

Mr Jon Fisk
Chief Executive Officer

Mr Wayne Honeywood
Chief Financial Officer

Website:
www.senteq.com.au

Sydney Airports Corporation Ltd

ACN: 082 578 809

Ansett and Sydney Airport have shared a remarkable place in Australia's aviation history. Sydney Airports Corporation Limited is proud to help Ansett celebrate its achievements at a time when Sydney Airport itself is celebrating 80 years of continuous operations. In partnership, we're creating world-class service in air travel for Australia.

Level 10
241 O'Riordan Street

Mascot NSW 2020

PO Box 63

Mascot NSW 1460

Phone: 61 2 9667 9111

Fax: 61 2 9667 1592

Mr David Mortimer
Chairman

Mr Tony Stuart
Chief Executive Officer

Website: www.sydney
airportmedia.com

Westralia Airports Corporation Pty Ltd

ACN: 077 153 130

Westralia Airports Corporation's vision is to be the most successful airport business in the world. Perth International Airport has a key role to play in Western Australia's economy, generating over $900 million annually in salaries and wages and approaching around 17,500 jobs. Westralia Airports Corporation congratulates Ansett Australia on its 65th anniversary.

Baker Road
(opposite domestic terminal)

Perth International
Airport WA 6105

PO Box 6

Cloverdale WA 6985

Phone: 61 8 9478 8888

Fax: 61 8 9277 7537

Mr Ross Beames
Chairman

Mr Graham Muir
Chief Executive Officer

Website:
www.perthairport.com
Email:
per@perthairport.net.au

WT Partnership

ACN: 006 040 768

WT Partnership is an international construction consultancy group specialising in Quantity Surveying, with an enviable track record for independent objective project cost management in successful property developments around the world. Our Ansett Australia alliance has kept construction costs in focus for over fifty years of developing building assets.

Level 4
390 St Kilda Road

Melbourne VIC 3004

Phone: 61 3 9867 3677

Fax: 61 3 9820 9224

Email:
wtpmelb@ocean.com.au

Mr Laurie Thomas
Chairman

Mr Ron Moir
Managing Director

about the chefs

The AWARENESS of

QUALITY INGREDIENTS

and the BIRTH of fusion

COOKING give Australia

not only the advantage

of PROMOTING the food

but also chefs who

provide the SPOTLIGHT

for the PRODUCE

to SHINE IN.

—*Simon Fenwick*

Stephanie Alexander OAM

Richmond Hill Cafe ♦ 48–50 Bridge Road ♦ Richmond ♦ Melbourne
Telephone 03 9421 2808

Stephanie Alexander has worked in the food industry as restaurateur, educator and writer for more than 25 years. She has published nine books, writes for several national food publications and in 1999 presented the ABC's six-part A Shared Table series.

Steve Baker

Executive Chef ♦ The Serai Hotel ♦ East Bali
Telephone 62 36 341 011

At The Serai Hotel, Steve Baker is responsible for all food and beverage operations and the hotel's cooking school.

Maggie Beer

Maggie Beer Farm Shop and Pheasant Farm Wine Sales
Pheasant Farm Road off Samuel Road ♦ Nuriootpa ♦ Barossa Valley
Telephone 08 8562 4477

Maggie and Colin Beer now operate an export kitchen in Tanunda producing pâté, verjuice, quince paste and other regional products for Australian and international markets.

Trevor Bilney

Manager Culinary Production
Bali Inter-Continental Resort on Jimbaran Beach ♦ Bali
Telephone 62 361 701 888

Trevor Bilney is responsible for the culinary production of six restaurants, four bars and lounges, and the Uluwatu Spa and Villa Retreats.

Tony Bilson

Ampersand ♦ The Roof Terrace ♦ Cockle Bay Wharf
201 Sussex Street ♦ Sydney
Telephone 02 9264 6666

Tony Bilson is involved in a wide range of consultancies and presently runs Ampersand restaurant and The Commissary Kitchen, a home meal replacement service.

Andrew Blake

Blakes ♦ Ground Level Southgate ♦ Southbank ♦ Melbourne
Telephone 03 9699 4100

Since Andrew Blake opened Blakes on the banks of the Yarra River in 1992, his menu and wine list have been at the cutting edge of the Melbourne food scene.

Guillaume Brahimi

Quay ♦ Overseas Passenger Terminal ♦ Circular Quay ♦ Sydney
Telephone 02 9241 4565

Guillaume Brahimi joined Bilson's (now Quay) in 1995. Quay has achieved Three Chefs Hats and was awarded Best French Restaurant in the 1999 *SMH Good Food Guide*.

James Brotherston & Antony Scholtmeyer

Jameson's ♦ 475 Adelaide Street ♦ Brisbane
Telephone 07 3831 7633

James Brotherston and Antony Scholtmeyer source produce Australia-wide to create dishes for Jameson's renowned for their flavour and texture.

Marieke Brugman

Howqua Dale Gourmet Retreat ♦ Howqua River Road via Mansfield
Telephone 03 5777 3503

Howqua Dale, Victoria, established in 1977 as a gourmet getaway, also includes a residential cooking school and organises gourmet tours.

Robert Castellani

Donovans ♦ 40 Jacka Boulevarde ♦ St Kilda ♦ Melbourne
Telephone 03 9534 8221

Robert Castellani began his apprenticeship at Fanny's Restaurant then moved to Stephanie's, where he worked for 7 years. He is Head Chef of Donovans.

Justin Connell

Inflight Chef ♦ Ansett International

Justin Connell served his apprenticeship at The Regent, Sydney, under Serge Dansereau, at Bilson's with Peter Kurvitz and at Jonah's.

Gary Cooper

Executive Chef ♦ Eleonore's Restaurant ♦ Chateau Yering
38–42 Melba Highway ♦ Yarra Valley
Telephone 03 9739 0111

Gary Cooper has been cooking his produce-driven menus in Victoria for more than 16 years. Eleonore's Restaurant was awarded Two Chefs Hats by the 1999 *The Age Good Food Guide*.

Andrew Cuthbert

Executive Chef ♦ Dubai Hilton ♦ Dubai Hilton Beach Club ♦ Dubai
Fax 971 4 313 383

Andrew Cuthbert worked at the Hilton in Melbourne and Gatwick before moving to Dubai in 1992, where he works with suppliers to provide hotel guests with quality Australian produce.

James Doherty

Inflight Chef ♦ Ansett International

James Doherty trained in New South Wales then moved to Hayman Island.

Peter Doyle

Cicada ♦ 29 Challis Avenue ♦ Potts Point ♦ Sydney
Telephone 02 9358 1255

Bev and Peter Doyle opened their multi-award-winning Cicada restaurant in 1987. Affectionately known by his peers as the 'chef's chef', Peter is renowned for his consistently light, fresh and innovative cuisine.

Teage Ezard

Ezard at Adelphi Hotel ♦ 187 Flinders Lane ♦ Melbourne
Telephone 03 9639 6811

Award-winning Teage Ezard opened Ezard at Adelphi, where he serves his definitive 'Australian free-style' food, in July 1999.

Alain Fabrègues

The Loose Box ◆ 6825 Great Eastern Highway ◆ Mundaring
Telephone 08 9295 1787

Alain Fabrègues opened The Loose Box in 1980. He has been Chef of the Year four times and won the Salon Culinaire Gold Medal for nine consecutive years.

Simon Fenwick

Executive Chef ◆ The Sugar Club ◆ 21 Warwick Street ◆ London
Telephone 44 20 7437 7776

Simon Fenwick has worked with Marco Pierre White, Janni Kyritsis, Damien Pignolet, Dietmar Sawyere and Liam Tomlin. He received the Josephine Pignolet Young Chef of the Year Award in 1996.

Timothy Fisher & Lucio Galletto

Lucio's ◆ 47 Windsor Street ◆ Paddington ◆ Sydney
Telephone 02 9380 5996

Lucio Galletto opened Lucio's in Balmain in 1981 and moved it to Paddington in 1983. Timothy Fisher joined Lucio's in 1994, becoming Executive Chef in 1996. *The Art of Food at Lucio's* was published in 1999.

Sean Flakelar

Executive Chef ◆ Amanusa Resort ◆ Bali
Telephone 62 361 772 333

Sean Flakelar worked with Neil Perry, Paul Merrony and David Thompson in Sydney before moving to Amanusa, a boutique resort in Bali, in 1992.

Mark Haynes

Executive Chef ◆ Hotel Lindrum ◆ 26 Flinders Street ◆ Melbourne
Telephone 03 9668 1111

Mark Haynes oversees the culinary teams within Marriner Theatres, Federici Cafe, Box Restaurant and Hotel Lindrum.

Michael Hoyle

Chef de Cuisine ◆ Breezes ◆ Crown ◆ Melbourne

In his three years at Eyton on the Yarra Winery restaurant, Michael Hoyle secured three Victorian tourism awards. Inspired by his passion for regional produce, he was instrumental in setting up Yarra Valley Food Group, which introduces food producers to chefs.

Simon Humble

Scusa Mi ◆ Mid-level Southgate ◆ Southbank ◆ Melbourne
Telephone 03 9699 4111

Scusa Mi's Simon Humble is regarded in Italy as one of their own, and is respected throughtout Australia for the integrity and presentation of his food.

Philip Johnson

e'cco ◆ corner Boundary Street & Adelaide Street ◆ Brisbane
Telephone 07 3831 8344

Philip Johnson has been a presence on the Brisbane restaurant scene since 1980. He opened e'cco in 1995. In 1997 e'cco was awarded *Australian Gourmet Traveller's* Restaurant of the Year. Since 1998, Philip has been a consultant chef for Air New Zealand.

Gary Jones

Jones ◆ 26 Dennis Street ◆ Subiaco
Telephone 08 9388 1585

Gary Jones' career includes working in restaurants and hotels throughout Europe and in Australia. He is currently owner, manager and chef of Jones.

Werner Kimmeringer

National Executive Chef ◆ Ansett Australia

Werner Kimmeringer had extensive experience in Europe before moving to The Hilton International in Sydney and Melbourne in 1985. He joined Ansett Australia in 1996 and has won numerous Salon Culinaire awards.

David King

Executive Chef ◆ Begawan Giri Estate ◆ Bali
Telephone 62 361 978 889

David King has worked in Sydney, San Francisco, London, Paris and Hong Kong. He has contributed to *marie claire*, *Vogue* and *Gourmet Traveller* and took part in the *Greatest Chefs of the World* series.

Allan Koh

Koko Restaurant ◆ Crown ◆ Melbourne

Allan Koh came to Australia in 1987 and was part of the opening team at Santori in Melbourne before joining Chinois in 1989, where he was chef de cuisine for six years. In 1997 he joined Crown as chef de cuisine.

Janni Kyritsis

MG Garage Restaurant ◆ 490 Crown Street ◆ Surry Hills ◆ Sydney
Telephone 02 9383 9383

Janni Kyritsis's CV includes Stephanie's, Berowra Waters Inn and the Bennelong Restaurant. His MG Garage, opened in November 1997, combines fine dining with a car showroom and was awarded Three Chefs Hats in the 1998 and 1999 *SMH Good Food Guide* awards.

Michael Lambie

Circa, The Prince ◆ 2 Ackland Street ◆ St Kilda ◆ Melbourne
Telephone 03 9536 1122

Michael Lambie worked with the Roux Brothers and Marco Pierre White in England before moving to Australia. Circa, The Prince, was named Best New Restaurant for 1998–99 by *The Age Good Food Guide* and awarded Three Chefs Hats.

David Laris

Oscar's Bar, Café and Restaurants ◆ Hong Kong
Telephone 852 2804 6561

At Oscars, Executive Chef David Laris has been responisble for introducing a modern Australian menu and developing the outside catering department. He also heads event management.

Ki Wah Lau

Silks Restaurant ◆ Crown ◆ Melbourne

Ki Wah Lau spent his formative cooking training years in Hong Kong, before moving to Melbourne in 1988. He joined Crown in 1997.

Cheong Liew OAM

The Grange ◆ Adelaide Hilton ◆ 233 Victoria Square ◆ Adelaide
Consultant Chef ◆ Parmelia Hilton ◆ Perth
Telephone 08 8217 2000

Cheong Liew's culinary brilliance has made him one of Adelaide's treasures and, according to the US *Wine & Food* magazine, he is one of the 10 'hottest chefs alive'.

Geoff Lindsay

Stella at Heide ◆ Museum of Modern Art ◆ Bulleen
Telephone 03 9852 1406

Geoff Lindsay opened Stella in 1994, is featured in New York's James Beard Foundation Directory, writes books, contributes to *The Australian* and regularly works as a guest chef in Australia and overseas.

Sean Macdougall

Executive Chef ◆ Park Hyatt Johannesburg
Telephone 27 11 280 1211

Since 1982, Sean Macdougall has worked in hotels in Australia, Europe, North America and Asia. He was transferred to the Park Hyatt Johannesburg in 1998.

Grant MacPherson

Executive Chef ◆ Bellagio Resort ◆ Las Vegas
Telephone 1 702 693 8186

Grant MacPherson oversees a staff of 860 along with the daily operations of 20 food and beverage outlets for the Bellagio Resort's US$200 million-a-year operation.

Christine Manfield
Paramount ◆ 73 Macleay Street ◆ Potts Point ◆ Sydney
Telephone 02 9358 1652

Christine Manfield is well known as a food writer, has published three best-selling cook books, including *Christine Manfield's Spice Collection*, teaches and guest chefs around the world. Paramount has been awarded Two Chefs Hats every year since 1994 in the *SMH Good Food Guide*.

Stefano Manfredi
bel mondo ◆ Level 3 ◆ The Argyle Department Store
12–24 Argyle Street ◆ The Rocks ◆ Sydney
Telephone 02 9241 3700

Stefano Manfredi has owned and run award-winning restaurants since 1983, published his *Fresh from Italy* (Hodder and Stoughton 1993), teaches, contributes to *Australian Gourmet Traveller* and is regularly invited to guest chef overseas.

Michael Mangan
Executive Chef ◆ Parkroyal ◆ Jalan Sultan Ismail ◆ Kuala Lumpur
Telephone 603 247 2381

Michael Mangan has worked with Hermann Schneider at Two Faces, run his own restaurant, Mangans, and worked in Australia, Europe and Asia. He joined Parkroyal Kuala Lumpur in 1998.

Thomas Milligan
Chef de Cuisine ◆ JJ's Bar & Grill ◆ Crown ◆ Melbourne

Thomas Milligan's Melbourne culinary career began as chef de cuisine of Stephanie's. At Crown he is chef de cuisine of JJ's Bar & Grill and responsible for Crown's room service operation.

Marcus Moore
Executive Chef ◆ Hotel Sofitel ◆ Melbourne
Telephone 03 9653 0000

Marcus Moore is responsible for Hotel Sofitel's five outlets and eight conference rooms. Le Restaurant was awarded Three Chefs Hats by *The Age Good Food Guide* from 1997 to 1999.

Geoffrey Nocher
Beach House Restaurant ◆ Hamilton Island

The Beach House is Hamilton Island's signature restaurant. Geoffrey Nocher is Beach Club Services Manager, overseeing the restaurant as well as Hamilton Island's new five-star boutique hotel.

Marcel Nosari
Executive Chef ◆ Hayman

Marcel Nosari, with extensive experience at restaurants and hotels throughout Europe and Australia, returned to Hayman in 1999, having been Executive Sous Chef at this award-winning resort from 1994 to 1997.

Anthony Papp
Inflight Chef ◆ Ansett International

Anthony Papp's varied experience ranges from fine dining rooms to large hotel brigades, consultancy work and corporate events.

Warren Pearson
Executive Chef ◆ Rosewood Hotels ◆ Riyadh
Telephone 966 1 465 4650

Responsible for the food and beverage makeover at this multi-outlet residential, hotel and commercial complex, Warren Pearson's role also includes coordinating royal functions and outside catering.

Andrew Phillips
Executive Chef ◆ Shangri-La Hotel ◆ Malaysia
Telephone 6 04 262 2622

Since completing training at Ryde Catering College in 1986, Andrew Phillips has worked in Australia, Canada and Hong Kong. He is presently responsible for all aspects of operation in this five-star hotel.

Graeme Phillips
19 Grays Road ◆ Ferntree ◆ Tasmania
Fax 03 6239 1741

Graeme Phillips recently sold his Battery Point Brasserie and now writes on wine for *The Mercury* and is working on a book on Tasmanian food.

Jacques Reymond
Jacques Reymond Restaurant ◆ 78 Williams Road ◆ Prahran ◆ Melbourne
Telephone 03 9525 2178

Jacques Reymond combines his French training with the finest Australian produce. His restaurant has won the prestigious Three Chefs Hats award from *The Age Good Food Guide* five years in a row.

Hermann Schneider
Arthurs ◆ Arthurs Seat Scenic Road ◆ Arthur's Seat ◆ Victoria
Telephone 03 5981 4444

Hermann Schneider sets standards by which others are judged. He came to Australia in 1956 as Chef of the French Olympic Team and stayed to open Two Faces in South Yarra (1960–87) and Arthurs in 1994.

Anders Schultz
Executive Chef ◆ Ansett International

After winning the Golden Chefs Hat, Anders travelled overseas to enhance his skills. He now develops Ansett's menus in conjunction with the inflight chefs and is in charge of day-to-day catering operations.

David Smith
Executive Chef ◆ Malolo Island ◆ Fiji
Telephone 679 722 607

With a CV that includes Armstrongs and The Regent Hotel, Sydney, David Smith is responsible for the food and beverage operations at Malolo Island Resort.

Craig Squire
Red Ochre Grill ◆ 43 Shields Street ◆ Cairns
Telephone 07 4051 0100

Craig Squire worked in Australia and Europe before setting up the Red Ochre Grill in Cairns, which is renowned for innovative techniques in creating stylish, modern dishes that incorporate native foods, in 1994.

Liam Tomlin
Executive Chef ◆ Banc and Wine Banc ◆ 53 Martin Place ◆ Sydney
Telephone 02 9233 5300

Liam Tomlin combines his role as Executive Chef at award-winning Banc with overseeing food for the Eaternity Group's operations at Wine Banc, Private Banc, Prime, and Post, at the new GPO Project at No.1 Martin Place.

John Torode
Smiths of Smithfield ◆ 67/77 Charterhouse Street ◆ London
Telephone 44 20 7236 6666

John Torode is widely known as the creator of the most distinctive food in the Conran Restaurant Group. His latest venture, Smiths of Smithfield, a four-floor restaurant and bar complex, opened recently and serves his trademark – simple foods with fantastic ingredients.

Scott Webster
Principal ◆ Australian Culinary Consultants Pty Ltd
Telephone 02 4961 4606

Scott Webster established Australian Culinary Consultants in 1989 to help Australian companies in the worldwide food service market. He is consultant to The Westin (No. 1 Martin Place, Sydney) and recently opened Restaurant Mosaic in the same complex.

Paul Wilson
The Chef ◆ Radii Restaurant & Bar ◆ Park Hyatt Melbourne

The former executive chef at Quaglino's, London, and Georges, Melbourne, is now at the award-winning Radii Restaurant & Bar, which was awarded Two Chefs Hats after only four months of trading and is home of *The Age Good Food Guide* Dish of the Year Award.

acknowledgements

Focus Publishing would like to thank the
following chefs for kindly granting permission
to include their recipes in this book.

Stephanie Alexander	33
Steve Baker	52
Maggie Beer	84, 106
Trevor Bilney	156
Tony Bilson	170
Andrew Blake	164
Guillaume Brahimi	40
James Brotherston	114
Marieke Brugman	126
Robert Castellani	122
Justin Connell	136
Gary Cooper	130, 162
Andrew Cuthbert	116
James Doherty	64
Peter Doyle	66, 168
Teage Ezard	138
Alain Fabrègues	48, 72
Simon Fenwick	42, 88
Timothy Fisher	44
Sean Flakelar	24
Lucio Galletto	44
Mark Haynes	68
Michael Hoyle	102
Simon Humble	70
Philip Johnson	104
Gary Jones	158
Werner Kimmeringer	154
David King	26
Allan Koh	78
Janni Kyritsis	50, 108
Michael Lambie	118
David Laris	120
Ki Wah Lau	86
Cheong Liew	124
Geoff Lindsay	82
Sean Macdougall	36
Grant MacPherson	76
Christine Manfield	74, 142
Stefano Manfredi	46, 56
Michael Mangan	160
Thomas Milligan	94
Marcus Moore	147
Geoffrey Nocher	58
Marcel Nosari	28
Anthony Papp	140
Warren Pearson	90
Andrew Phillips	100
Graeme Phillips	80
Jacques Reymond	30
Hermann Schneider	92
Antony Scholtmeyer	114
Anders Schultz	22
David Smith	110
Craig Squire	38
Liam Tomlin	112, 144
John Torode	166
Scott Webster	128
Paul Wilson	150

We would like to thank the Star Alliance
Partners for providing recipes and images
for the Star Alliance chapter.

The publisher would like to thank Foodservice
Equipment International Pty Limited for their
generosity in supplying the wonderful china,
glassware and cutlery, and Cicada Restaurant
for their kind help in providing additional props.

photo credits

page 14 James Halliday, pages 19–20,
132–133, 172–173 IPL Image Group,
pages 96–97 Tourism Victoria.